SO-AAB-614

Jesus Is Born
Jesus' Miracles
Zaccheus

Group's hands-On BiBLE curriculum™

Preschool
Winter
Teachers Guide

Group
Loveland, Colorado

Group

Hands-On Bible Curriculum™, Preschool, Winter
Copyright © 1995 Group Publishing, Inc.

Second Printing, 1997

All rights reserved. No part of this book may be reproduced in any manner whatsoever without prior written permission from the publisher, except where noted on handouts and in the case of brief quotations embodied in critical articles and reviews. For information write Permissions, Group Publishing, Inc., Dept. BK, P.O. Box 481, Loveland, CO 80539.

Credits
Contributing Authors: Barbie Murphy, Jennifer Nystrom, and Bonnie Temple
Editors: Jennifer Root Wilger and Jody Brolsma
Senior Editor: Lois Keffer
Chief Creative Officer: Joani Schultz
Copy Editor: Janis Sampson
Art Director: Lisa Chandler
Cover Art Director: Helen H. Lannis
Designers: Lisa Chandler and Jean Bruns
Computer Graphic Artist: Bill Fisher
Cover Photographer: Craig DeMartino
Illustrators: Shelley Dieterichs, Joan Holub, Megan Jeffery, and Judy Love
Audio Engineer: Steve Saavedra
Production Manager: Gingar Kunkel

Unless otherwise noted, Scriptures quoted from The Youth Bible, New Century Version, copyright © 1991 by Word Publishing, Dallas, Texas 75039. Used by permission.

ISBN 0-7644-0057-6
Printed in the United States of America.

# Contents

Which Age Level of Group's® Toddlers Through 6-Year-Olds Hands-On Bible Curriculum™ Is Right for Your Class?

Maximize your teaching success by choosing the curriculum that's best suited to the needs of the children you teach. With preschoolers, a few months can make a big difference in what works in the classroom and what doesn't! This overview shows how Group's® **Hands-On Bible Curriculum™ for Toddlers Through 6-Year-Olds** carefully tracks with developmental guidelines.

Toddlers & 2s

- colorful three-dimensional Interactive StoryBoards™ with sensory items for children to touch, taste, and smell
- supervised play centers
- emphasis on large motor skills
- simple rhymes and finger plays
- repetition and encouragement
- simple questions and responses

Preschool, 3s & 4s

- an exciting variety of Bible-story tools, including Learning Mats™, Jumbo Bible Puzzles™, *Bible Big Books*™, and Fold-Out Learning Mats™
- guided options in "Let's Get Started" and "For Extra Time"
- side-by-side play
- age-appropriate craft ideas that don't require cutting
- simple interaction using pair-shares and assembly-lines

Pre-K & K, 5s & 6s

- Bible stories with more depth based on Learning Mats™, *Bible Big Books*™, Jumbo Bible Puzzles™, and Fold-Out Learning Mats™
- more individual choices and independent learning activities
- thought-provoking questions
- more challenging craft activities
- more frequent use of interactive learning

Of course, *every* age level of **Hands-On Bible Curriculum for Toddlers Through 6-Year-Olds** includes

- exciting, easy-to-prepare lessons
- a cassette of lively songs that teach
- photocopiable take-home papers to help parents reinforce Bible truths at home
- a solid biblical point in language young children can understand
- memorable five-senses learning carefully tied to the Bible truth
- big, bright, exciting Bible art
- interaction with a puppet friend who learns from the children
- options that allow you to customize each lesson for your class

Choose the age level that most closely matches your students' needs, then teach with confidence, knowing that you're providing the optimum learning environment for the little ones God has entrusted to your care.

How to Use This Book

Welcome to Hands-On Bible Curriculum™

There's nothing more rewarding than helping young children know, love, and follow Jesus Christ. But getting the message across to preschoolers can be a challenge! Three- and 4-year-olds aren't ready to absorb abstract theological concepts, but they can certainly understand that Jesus loves and cares for them.

Hands-On Bible Curriculum for Preschool presents simple Bible truths in a fresh, interactive setting that capitalizes on children's need to experience life with all their senses. With *Group's Bible Big Books™* and *Group's Learning Mat™*, you'll help children discover Bible lessons in creative, active ways that will capture their attention and keep them coming back for more.

Each Hands-On Bible Curriculum lesson for preschool is based on an important Bible story. Each lesson's Point distills the Bible story into a simple, memorable Bible truth 3- and 4-year-olds can understand and experience.

Active Learning: What I Do, I Learn

Group's Hands-On Bible Curriculum uses a unique approach to Christian education called active learning. In each session children participate in a variety of fun and memorable learning experiences that help them understand one important Point.

Research shows that kids remember about 90 percent of what they do, but less than 10 percent of what they hear. The 3- and 4-year-olds in your class learn best by doing, smelling, tasting, feeling, hearing, and seeing. They need to be actively involved in lively experiences that bring home the lesson's Point.

With active learning, the teacher becomes a guide, pointing the way for the learner to discover Bible truths through hands-on experiences. Instead of filling little minds with facts, you'll participate alongside your students in the joy of discovery, then carefully summarize each Bible truth.

Don't be alarmed if your classroom seems a little noisier with active learning! Having quiet and controlled students doesn't necessarily mean your class is a success. A better clue might be seeing happy, involved, excited children moving around the classroom, discovering Bible truths with all their senses.

In order to succeed with active learning, you'll need an attention-getting signal. An attention-getting signal such as flashing the lights or raising your hand will let children know it's time to stop what they're doing and look at you. Each week remind the children about your signal and practice it together. Soon, regaining their attention will become a familiar classroom ritual.

Interactive Learning: Together We Learn Better

From their earliest years, children learn from interacting with people around them. Bolstered by the encouragement of parents and friends, they try, then fail, then try again until they learn to walk, talk, run, write—the list goes on and on. Because children truly want to learn, they keep seeking help from those around them until they master a concept or skill.

Children don't learn in isolation. Interactive learning comes naturally to young children. So why not put its benefits to work in the church?

In Hands-On Bible Curriculum, children work together to discover and explore Bible truths. The interactive Bible lessons also help children learn kindness, patience, and cooperation. As they assume unique roles and participate in group learning activities, children discover firsthand that church is a place where everyone can belong, and no one is left out.

Like active learning, interactive learning may produce a bit more noise than you're used to. Sometimes you may feel like you've lost control. But you haven't really lost it—you've just allowed the children to take ownership of their learning. With interactive learning, you won't have to prod or nag students to learn—they'll be motivated by the joy of discovery. Try it, you'll like it!

Use the following guidelines to help make interactive learning work for your class:

● **Establish guidelines for acceptable behavior.** Invite the children to help you create classroom rules. Rules that work well with 3- and 4-year-olds include: Use quiet voices, stay at your workplace, work together, help each other, and say nice words to others. Children will enjoy reminding each other to follow rules they've helped create.

● **Use paired instruction.** Pair up children with similar abilities during activities. When you ask a question, have children ask that question of their partners.

● **Assign specific tasks to individuals working in groups.** When children work in groups of more than two, each child should be assigned a unique and important task. To help children remember their tasks, consider using colored necklaces, headbands, or badges. If you're making sandwiches, for example, children with red badges could be in charge of bread, children with green badges could be in charge of peanut butter, and children with blue badges could be in charge of jelly.

● **Discuss each activity with the children.** Ask children to tell you what they did, and what they liked and didn't like about it. Invite them to share their learning discoveries with you and with other groups. Praise groups that seemed to work together well, and soon other groups will follow their example.

Learning Is an Exciting Adventure!

Let the Holy Spirit be your guide as you teach this quarter of Hands-On Bible Curriculum. With active and interactive learning, your students will enter a whole new world of Bible discovery. They'll be fascinated with *Group's Bible Big Book, Group's Learning Mats, rubber stamps,* and other learning materials in the Learning Lab®. And you'll feel good about seeing children enjoy these important Bible lessons.

Sound exciting? Let's walk through a lesson and discover how Hands-On Bible Curriculum for Preschool will work for you.

The Point

● **The Point contains the one important Bible truth children will learn in each lesson.** Each Point is carefully worded in simple language that 3- and 4-year-olds can easily understand and remember. Each activity reinforces The Point. You can find The Point by looking for the pointing-pencil icon that accompanies The Point each time it occurs in the text.

● **Be sure to repeat The Point as it's written each time it appears.** You may feel you're being redundant, but you're actually helping children remember an important Bible truth. Studies show people need to hear new information up to 75 times to learn it. Repetition is a good thing—especially for 3- and 4-year-olds. So remember to repeat The Point as you sum up each activity.

The Bible Basis

● **The Bible Basis gives you background information you'll need to teach the lesson.** The first paragraph provides details and background for the lesson's Bible story. Read the Bible story ahead of time to familiarize yourself with key details. The second paragraph tells how the story and Point relate to 3- and 4-year-olds. Use the developmental information in this paragraph to help you anticipate children's responses.

This Lesson at a Glance

● **The Lesson at a Glance chart gives you a quick overview of the lesson and lists supplies you'll need for each activity.** Most of the supplies are items you already have readily available in your home or classroom. Simplify your preparation by choosing which Let's Get Started and For Extra Time activities you'll use. Then gather only the supplies you'll need for those activities and the main body of the lesson.

Take time to familiarize yourself with the Learning Lab items. Read the *Bible Big Books,* unfold the *Learning Mat,* listen to the *cassette tape,* stamp with the *rubber stamps.* Pray for your 3- and 4-year-olds as you have fun preparing.

Welcome!

● **Your class begins each week with a time to greet children and welcome them to class.** Three- and 4-year-olds may still feel anxious about leaving their parents, so your welcoming presence is important! If children see you smiling at the door week after week, they'll soon offer you their trust and look forward to coming to class.

● **When you meet the children in your class for the first time, call them by name.** Introduce yourself to parents and let them know you're glad to be teaching their children. Help children make name tags using the patterns provided on page 30. Consider laminating the name tags after the first week so they'll last the entire quarter. Fasten the name tags to children's clothing using tape or safety pins. Children will enjoy wearing name tags they've made themselves, and you'll find yourself referring to the name tags often when you can't quite remember all the children's names.

● **Model Christ's love to your students by bending down to their**

level when you listen or speak to them. Be sure to make eye contact, hold a hand, pat a shoulder, and say each child's name some time during the morning. Take a few moments to find out how each child is feeling before leading children into your first lesson activity.

Let's Get Started

● **Let's Get Started involves children right away in meaningful activities related to the lesson.** Each lesson provides you with several optional activities for children to do as they arrive. You can choose to do one or more of them. These activities prepare children for the lesson they'll be learning and provide them with opportunities for positive social interaction.

● **Set up appropriate areas in your classroom to accommodate each activity.** Let's Get Started activities range from blocks and fine-motor manipulatives to dramatic play with dress-up clothing and props to arts and crafts. Allow plenty of space in each activity area for children to have freedom of movement.

Three and 4-year-olds use dramatic play to try on roles and process what they know and feel about relationships and the world around them. Set out small dishes and cups, a small table, and typical toy kitchen appliances. If your budget is limited, ask a parent to make play furniture out of wood, or use sturdy cardboard boxes. Dolls, blankets, and a doll bed are important elements in an early childhood classroom.

Provide dress-up clothing that represents male and female roles, as well as items that reflect children's culture. You can also gather bathrobes and towels to use as Bible-time costumes. Avoid adult pants or other clothing that might cause children to trip and fall. If your church doesn't have a collection of dress-up clothes, consider asking parents or church members to donate old clothes, hats, purses, and briefcases. Dress-up clothes can also be purchased inexpensively at second-hand stores.

If you use tables, make sure they're child-sized. Forcing children to work at adult-sized tables can cause spills, messes, and even accidents. If your church doesn't have child-sized furniture or if you're meeting in a nontraditional space, set up art or manipulative activities on the floor. Trays, shallow boxes, or dishpans can be used to hold the items needed for the lesson. Use masking tape to mark off the area and cover the floor with newspaper or a plastic tablecloth. Consider using crates or cement blocks to hold up an adult-sized table top with its legs collapsed.

● **Make Let's Get Started work for your class!** Depending on the number of children and adult helpers you have, set up one, two, or all of the activities. Station an adult at each activity area and run several activities simultaneously, or lead all children in one activity at a time. If you want to move quickly into Bible-Story Time, pick one Let's Get Started activity. If you often have latecomers, plan to use more activities.

● **Always discuss each Let's Get Started activity with the children.** Let's Get Started activities allow children to explore The Point independently in a casual setting. Talking with children about these activities helps them make an important faith connection. For example, 3- and 4-year-olds may love playing at a nature table, but they won't connect it with a loving creator God without your help. Circulate among the areas to guide activities and direct children's conversation toward the lesson. As you have the opportunity, repeat The Point.

● **Vary the activities you use.** Remember that children learn in different ways. The more senses you can involve, the more they'll learn. By including a variety of Let's Get Started activities each quarter, you'll be able to reach children of all learning styles and developmental abilities.

Pick-Up Song

● **Sing the Pick-Up Song when you're ready to move on to the Bible-Story Time.** Singing helps young children make a smooth transition to the next activity. Your Pick-Up Song is "Now It's Time," sung to the tune of "The Mulberry Bush." Shortly before you start singing, tell children that it's almost time to clean up. If you're uncomfortable with singing, use the *cassette tape* or ask a volunteer to help you. At first, children will just listen to the song, but they'll quickly catch on and sing along. Soon, cleaning up the room will become a familiar ritual that children actually enjoy!

Bible-Story Time

● **Introduce and review the attention-getting signal.** Attention-getting signals help you stay in control. Use the signal described in the lessons to let children know it's time to stop what they're doing and look at you.

● **Use "Setting the Stage" to formally introduce The Point and set up the Bible-story action.** To wrap up Let's Get Started, have children tell you what they did and formally connect their experiences to The Point. Then complete the "Setting the Stage" activity to lead children from The Point to the Bible story. Even though The Point is tied to the Bible story, most 3- and 4-year-olds won't make the connection. The summary statement at the end of the activity will help you provide children with a clear transition.

● **Use "Bible Song and Prayer Time" to teach children to love and respect God's Word.** Choose a special Bible to use for this section of the lesson each week. For example, you could use a big, black Bible; a red Bible; or a Bible with gold leaf pages. These special characteristics will make Bible time memorable for the children. Even though you'll be using *Group's Bible Big Book* and *Group's Learning Mats* to tell the Bible story, be sure to tell children that the story comes from the Bible, God's Word. The Bible Song provided in the lesson and on the *cassette tape* each week will prepare children to focus on the Bible story.

● **Tell the Bible story with enthusiasm.** Read the Bible story and practice telling it before class. Think about voice changes, gestures and motions, and eye contact. Refer to the Teacher Tips in the Teachers Guide to help you. If you'll be using the *cassette tape* to tell the story, listen to it ahead of time.

Use questions in the Teachers Guide to draw children into discussions and help them focus on the Bible story. Invite children to help you tell the Bible story if they already know it. Listen to children's questions and responses, but don't let them steer you too far away from the story.

To refocus children when they become distracted, use a child's name and ask a direct question. You might say, "Julia, what do you think the shepherds thought when they saw the baby Jesus?"

● **Move on to "Do the Bible Story" quickly.** Most 3- and 4-year-olds have a 5- to 10-minute attention span. After they've been sitting for "Hear the Bible Story," they'll be ready to get up and move around. The "Do the Bible Story" section lets them jump up and wear out the wiggles without wiggling away from the lesson!

Practicing The Point

● **Practicing The Point lets children practice and teach what they've learned.** In this section, children interact with a puppet friend about The Point. You can use Whiskers the Mouse, available from Group Publishing, or any puppet of your choice. You can even make your own mouse puppet!

Whiskers is a little shy, so encourage children to approach him slowly and gently. Remind children that if they make Whiskers feel at home, he'll want to come back and visit them again. In spite of his shyness, Whiskers wants to be friends with the children and often needs their help to make good decisions.

You'll be amazed to discover how much your children have learned as they share the lesson with Whiskers. Even children who are shy around adults will open up to Whiskers. After several weeks, children will begin to expect Whiskers' regular visits and will be ready to share what they've learned.

For a change of pace, try one of the following ideas for bringing Whiskers into other parts of the lesson:
● Have Whiskers greet children as they arrive.
● Have children tell the Bible story to Whiskers.
● Have Whiskers participate in games or other activities.
● Have Whiskers ask questions to draw out shy children.
● Have Whiskers give the attention-getting signal.
● Have Whiskers encourage disruptive children to quiet down.
● Use Whiskers to snuggle or hug children.

You can purchase Whiskers in your local Christian bookstore or directly from Group Publishing by calling 1-800-447-1070.

Closing

● **The closing activity gives you an opportunity to repeat The Point once more and wrap up the class session.** As you complete the closing activity, encourage children to say The Point with you. Encourage them to share The Point with their families when they go home.

For Extra Time

● **If you have a long class period or simply want to add variety to your lessons, try one of the For Extra Time activities.** For Extra Time activities include learning games, crafts, and snacks related to the lesson, as well as suggestions to enhance each lesson's story picture. Most of these ideas could also be used in the Let's Get Started section of the lesson. Each For Extra Time activity lists the supplies you'll need.

Today I Learned . . .

● **The photocopiable "Today I Learned . . ." handout helps parents and children interact about the lesson.** Each handout includes a verse to learn, family activity ideas, a story picture, and an "Ask Me . . ." section with questions for parents to ask their children about the lesson. Encourage parents to use the handout to help them reinforce what their children are learning at church.

Understanding Your 3- and 4-Year-Olds

Physical Development

- Lots of energy.
- Walk and run with confidence.
- Drawings include recognizable shapes.
- Can work simple puzzles.

Emotional Development

- Generally happy.
- Influenced by the reactions of other children.
- Sensitive to the moods and reactions of adults.

Social Development

- Boys usually play with boys, girls with girls.
- Prefer short group experiences.
- Use language in dramatic play.

Mental Development

- Can recall some facts and events.
- Can memorize stories, songs, or finger plays.
- Ask lots of questions.
- Have an attention span of no longer than 10 minutes.

Spiritual Development

- Hear and enjoy Bible stories.
- Recognize own church; develop sense of belonging at church.
- Understand that prayer is talking to God; pray simple, spontaneous prayers.

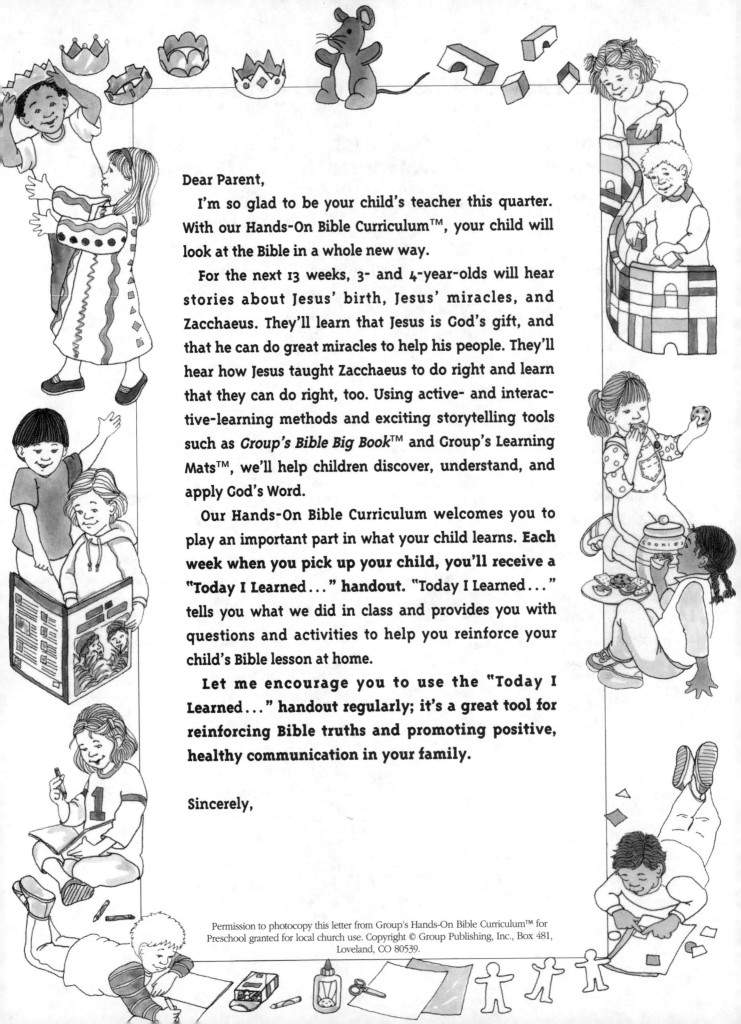

Dear Parent,

I'm so glad to be your child's teacher this quarter. With our Hands-On Bible Curriculum™, your child will look at the Bible in a whole new way.

For the next 13 weeks, 3- and 4-year-olds will hear stories about Jesus' birth, Jesus' miracles, and Zacchaeus. They'll learn that Jesus is God's gift, and that he can do great miracles to help his people. They'll hear how Jesus taught Zacchaeus to do right and learn that they can do right, too. Using active- and interactive-learning methods and exciting storytelling tools such as *Group's Bible Big Book*™ and Group's Learning Mats™, we'll help children discover, understand, and apply God's Word.

Our Hands-On Bible Curriculum welcomes you to play an important part in what your child learns. Each week when you pick up your child, you'll receive a "Today I Learned..." handout. "Today I Learned..." tells you what we did in class and provides you with questions and activities to help you reinforce your child's Bible lesson at home.

Let me encourage you to use the "Today I Learned..." handout regularly; it's a great tool for reinforcing Bible truths and promoting positive, healthy communication in your family.

Sincerely,

Permission to photocopy this letter from Group's Hands-On Bible Curriculum™ for Preschool granted for local church use. Copyright © Group Publishing, Inc., Box 481, Loveland, CO 80539.

Jesus Is Born

The most important person ever to come into the world came not as a conquering king, but as a tiny, helpless infant. God's Son was born not in a high-tech hospital with the world's best attending physicians, not in the comfort of a warm and safe home, not in a castle with trumpets and fanfare fitting for a king. Instead, Jesus was born in a simple stable, probably a cave used to house domestic animals. Only Mary, Joseph, and perhaps a few animals attended his birth. This was the package in which God sent the precious gift of his only Son.

Three- and 4-year-olds love the celebration of Christmas with its glittery decorations and enticing packages, the special foods that fill our tables, and the hospitality shared with family and friends. It takes extra effort to bring our children past the glitter, the gifts, and the abundance to the true meaning of Christmas. Use these lessons to demonstrate the wonder of Jesus' coming and to point them to the true meaning of Christmas—the arrival of Jesus, God's promised Savior and the most special gift of all.

Five Lessons on Jesus Is Born

	Page	The Point	Bible Basis
Lesson 1 A Special Message	19	The angel told Mary that Jesus is God's special gift.	Luke 1:26-38
Lesson 2 The Most Special Gift	33	Jesus is God's special gift.	Luke 2:1-7
Lesson 3 Just a Shepherd	45	The shepherds were glad that Jesus is God's special gift.	Luke 2:8-15
Lesson 4 Praising the Savior	59	Jesus is God's special gift, and we worship him.	Luke 2:15-20
Lesson 5 Gifts of Love	73	Jesus is God's special gift, and we love him.	Matthew 2:1-12

Time Stretchers

Born for You and Me

● **The Point**

Gather the children around you. Say: ●**Jesus is God's special gift to each of us. When you hear your name called, come and hold hands and form a circle with me. Let's start. Jesus is God's special gift to** (name) **and** (name).

Invite the children you named to come to you and join hands. Continue to say: **Jesus is God's special gift to** (name) **and** (name) until you've named all the children, and your circle is complete. Then walk around in a circle as you sing this song, to the tune of "The Farmer's in the Dell."

Sing

Jesus was born for you.
Jesus was born for me.
Jesus was born in Bethlehem,
Born for you and me.

● **The Point**

Repeat the song and insert children's names in place of "you" and "me." Close the activity by having children repeat The Point together: ●Jesus is God's special gift.

A Spinning Gift

Before class, wrap up a box of treats such as Christmas cookies or graham crackers. Make sure you include enough treats for each child to have one.

● **The Point**

Have children sit together in a circle. Place an empty 2-liter plastic soft drink bottle in the center of the circle. Say: **Today we're learning that ●Jesus is God's special gift. To help us learn about that, I brought a special gift for us today. But before we open it, we're going to play a game. I'll spin this bottle, and whoever it points to when it stops will get to hold the gift and say, ●"Jesus is God's special gift." Let's all try saying that now. ●Jesus is God's special gift.**

● **The Point**

After a while, I'll stop spinning the bottle, and we'll get to open the gift. But you won't know when—it will be a surprise.

Spin the bottle several times. Each time the bottle stops, encourage the child it's pointing to to say, "Jesus is God's special gift" as he or she accepts the gift box. After most children have had a turn, stand the bottle up.

Say: **Surprise! It's time to open our special gift.**

● **The Point**

Give the gift to a child who hasn't had a turn holding it yet and then continue: ●**Jesus is God's special gift. People didn't know when Jesus would come, just as we didn't know when we'd get to open our special gift today. Let's open it now and see what's inside.**

Have the child (and those around him or her) unwrap the gift and give everyone a treat from inside. As children enjoy their treats, say: **We're having a**

● **The Point**

special treat today to celebrate Jesus' birth. ●Jesus is God's special gift.

Remembering God's Word

Each four- or five-week module focuses on a key Bible verse. The key verse for this module is "My heart rejoices in God my Savior" (Luke 1:47).

This module's key verse will teach children that loving Jesus makes us happy. Have fun using these ideas any time during the lessons on Jesus' birth.

My Heart Rejoices

Say: **There's a verse in our Bible that tells us how Mary felt about being Jesus' mother. Listen while I read it to you.**

Open your Bible to Luke 1:47 and read the sentence aloud to the children. Have children repeat the verse with you and then say: **Mary said that her heart was rejoicing—that means she felt really happy inside.** Ask:

● **When have you felt really happy inside?** (When I got a good Christmas present; when it was my birthday; when I went to the park.)

● **What do you do when you're happy?** (Smile; play; laugh.)

Say: **Mary was so happy that Jesus was coming. We can be happy about Jesus, too. I have a song we can sing to help us learn this verse.**

Lead children in singing "My Heart Rejoices" with the *cassette tape,* to the tune of "Ten Little Indians." The song is recorded twice. Children can listen the first time, then sing along as they begin to learn the words.

Sing

My heart re-joices.
My heart re-joices.
My heart re-joices
In God my Savior!

(Repeat twice)

Once children have learned the song, have them join hands and move around in a circle as they sing the song.

Happy Hearts

Before class, prepare white hearts by folding sheets of paper in half and cutting, as shown in the margin illustration. You'll need two hearts for each child in your class.

Give each child two hearts. Have children draw a happy face on one heart and a sad face on the other heart. As children work, have them tell you about times they've felt happy and times they've felt sad. Help children post their finished heart faces around the room.

Say: **Show me how you look when you feel sad inside.** Pause. **Now show me how you look when you feel happy inside.** Pause. **I'm going to read some things that might make you feel happy or sad. If I read something that makes you feel happy, go stand by your happy heart. If I read something that makes you feel sad, go stand by your sad heart.**

Read the following list. Pause after you read each item to allow time for children to find their hearts.

● **Your favorite toy is broken.**

- **Your family goes out for ice cream.**
- **Your friend comes over to play.**
- **You have to stay home from a birthday party because you're sick.**
- **You get a new toy.**
- **You get to open your Christmas presents.**

Say: **We're happy at Christmas because we get to do so many fun things. We get to decorate Christmas trees, eat yummy Christmas treats, and open presents from our friends and families. Those are all good things to be happy about. But do you know the best thing to be happy about at Christmas? Christmas is Jesus' birthday, and** **Jesus is God's special gift. When Mary found out that she was going to be Jesus' mother, she was so happy, she said that her heart was rejoicing. Listen to this Bible verse.**

✏ The Point

Read the key verse aloud and then have children repeat it with you.

Say: **Let's whisper the verse quietly, like it's a secret we're happy and excited about.**

Lead children in whispering the verse. Then say: **Now let's jump up and shout the verse loudly, like we're so happy and excited we want to tell everybody about Jesus.**

Lead children in shouting the verse, then say: **Remember to be happy about Jesus' birth this Christmas.**

Story Enhancements

Make Bible lessons come alive in your classroom by bringing Bible costumes, setting out sensory items that fit with the story, or creating exciting bulletin boards to stimulate interest. The following ideas will help get you started.

The Giving Box

Before you teach this module, contact a local homeless shelter or family crisis center. Explain that the children in your class would like to share a gift with the children at the shelter or center and ask what they might need. Fill in and photocopy the parent letter (p. 18) explaining your project. Send the letter home with children.

Set out a class giving box where children can see it. Show the box to the children and explain that you'll be filling it with food and toys to share with other children who need them. Let children decorate the box with Christmas gift wrap or garland or stamp the box with the *angel stamp*. As children decorate the box, talk about what kinds of things they can bring to share.

Each week have children add to the box. Let them touch and hold the items if they're interested. As children put their items in the box, talk about how they'll be giving a special Christmas gift to boys and girls who don't have special things at Christmastime.

At the end of the module, make arrangements to deliver your gifts.

TEACHER TIPS

✔ It's important that each child gets a chance to participate in this project. As you take things out of the box, encourage children who haven't brought anything to help you put them back in. You may also want to ask other church members to contribute extra canned food in case some children don't bring any.

Stable Time

Set up a simple stable by cutting a door in a large appliance box or draping a blanket over a table. Put a few stuffed animals in the stable along with a box or bed with a doll in it. Tell children that you'll have the stable set up each week. Encourage them to take turns playing in the stable and acting out the story of Jesus' birth.

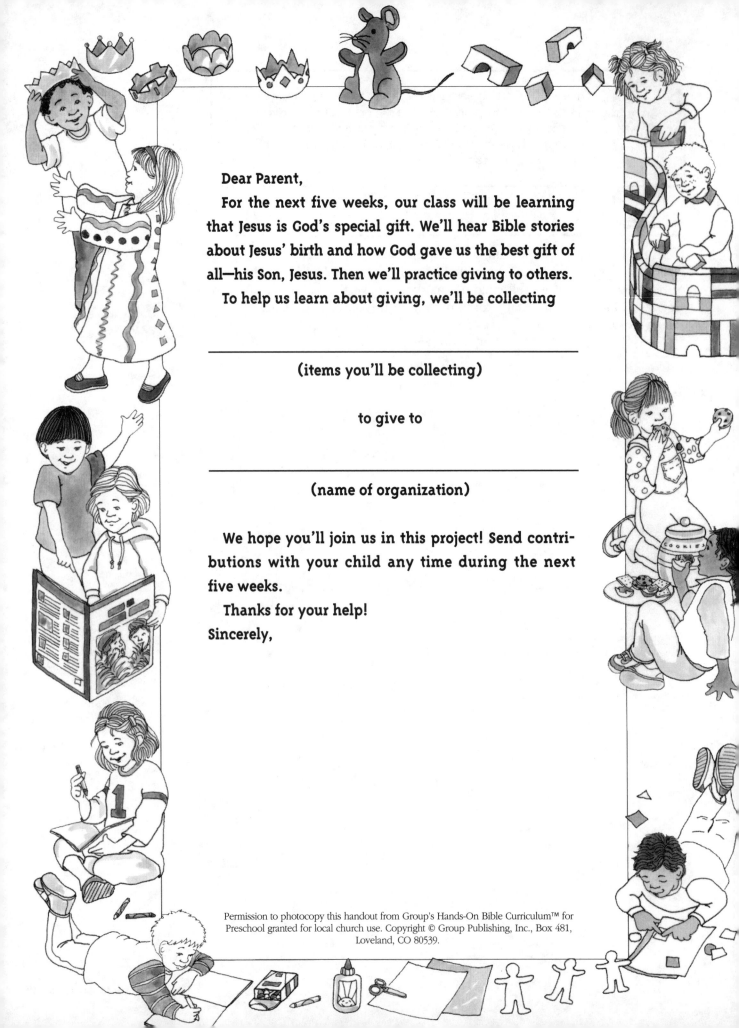

Dear Parent,

For the next five weeks, our class will be learning that Jesus is God's special gift. We'll hear Bible stories about Jesus' birth and how God gave us the best gift of all—his Son, Jesus. Then we'll practice giving to others.

To help us learn about giving, we'll be collecting

_____

(items you'll be collecting)

to give to

_____

(name of organization)

We hope you'll join us in this project! Send contributions with your child any time during the next five weeks.

Thanks for your help!

Sincerely,

Permission to photocopy this handout from Group's Hands-On Bible Curriculum™ for Preschool granted for local church use. Copyright © Group Publishing, Inc., Box 481, Loveland, CO 80539.

A Special Message

The Bible Basis

Luke 1:26-38. The angel comes to Mary.

It happened on a day like any other. Mary was tending her daily routine when an angel appeared before her. The message he brought sent her world spinning in confusion, surprise, and excitement. She was to be the mother of God's Son! Many questions must have filled Mary's mind, but the angel's words of comfort and encouragement filled her heart with wonder. Her spirit of faith rose to magnify the Lord, the God of the impossible, as she embraced God's remarkable plan.

Three- and 4-year-olds are sensitive to change. Statements such as "You're going to have a new brother or sister" "We're moving to a new home" or "This is your new baby sitter" mean big changes for little ones. Like Mary, children often feel a mixture of surprise, fear, and excitement at these times. Use this lesson to help children feel the excitement of a promised blessing and to recognize that Jesus is God's special gift to us.

Getting The Point

✎ **The angel told Mary that Jesus is God's special gift.**

It's important to say The Point just as it's written in each activity. Repeating The Point over and over will help the children remember it and apply it to their lives.

Children will
● talk about things that surprise them,
● surprise each other in a game,
● hear a story about something special that happened to Mary, and
● thank God for his special gift—Jesus.

✎ **The Point**

This Lesson at a Glance

Before the lesson, collect the necessary items for the activities you plan to use. Refer to the Classroom Supplies and Learning Lab Supplies columns to determine what you'll need. Remember to make photocopies of the "Today I Learned..." handout (p. 31) to send home with your children.

Section	Minutes	What Children Will Do	Classroom Supplies	Learning Lab Supplies
Welcome Time	up to 5	**Welcome!**—Receive name tags and be greeted by the teacher.	"Angel Name Tags" handouts (p. 30), marker, safety pins or tape	
Let's Get Started Direct children to one or more of the Let's Get Started activities until everyone arrives.	up to 10	**Option 1: Room Angels**—Make life-size angels to hang up around the room.	Newsprint, pencils or markers, scissors, tape	
	up to 10	**Option 2: Mary and Joseph Living Center**—Dress up and pretend they're Mary and Joseph.	Robes, towels, belts or string, scarves, toy dishes, broom, wooden blocks, toy tools	
	up to 10	**Option 3: Surprise Paintings**—Make a surprising painting and hear how Mary was surprised by an angel.	Tempera paint, white crayons, white paper, paintbrushes	
Pick-Up Song	up to 5	**Now It's Time**—Sing a song as they pick up toys and gather for Bible-Story Time.	Cassette player	Cassette: "Now It's Time"
Bible-Story Time	up to 8	**Setting the Stage**—Play a game to surprise each other.	Glitter glue	Gift box, gift bow
	up to 5	**Bible Song and Prayer Time**—Sing a song, bring out the Bible, and pray together.	Bible, cassette player	Angel stamp and ink pad, cassette: "We Are Glad..."
	up to 5	**Hear the Bible Story**—Hear how an angel appeared to Mary.	Bible	Learning Mat: Jesus' Birth
	up to 8	**Do the Bible Story**—Move to music and decorate the Learning Mat.	Cassette player, crayons, markers, glitter glue	Cassette: "Angel Music," Learning Mat
Practicing The Point	up to 5	**Surprise!**—Tell Whiskers about the angel who appeared to Mary.	Whiskers the Mouse	
Closing	up to 5	**Jesus Is God's Gift**—Stamp each other's hands to remind each other that Jesus is God's gift.		Angel stamp and ink pad
For Extra Time		For extra-time ideas and supplies, see page 29.		

Jesus is God's special gift.

Welcome Time

Welcome! (up to 5 minutes)

- Bend down and make eye contact with children as they arrive.
- Greet each child individually with an enthusiastic smile.
- Thank each child for coming to class today.
- Say: **Today we're going to learn that** the angel told Mary that **Jesus is God's special gift.**
- Give each child a photocopy of an angel name tag from page 30. Help children write their names on their name tags and pin or tape them to their clothing. You may want to cover the name tags with clear adhesive plastic so they'll last through the quarter.
- Direct children to the Let's Get Started activities you've set up.

The Point

Let's Get Started

Set up one or more of the following activities for children to do as they arrive. After you greet each child, invite him or her to choose an activity.

Circulate among the children to offer help as needed and direct children's conversation toward the point of today's lesson. Ask questions such as "Have you ever done something to surprise someone? Tell me about it" or "Tell me about a time when someone surprised you."

Option 1: Room Angels (up to 10 minutes)

Lay a large sheet of newsprint on the floor for each child. Have the children lie on the paper, arms held out, while you trace their body shapes. Trace each child from fingertip to fingertip, then from waist to ankle on each side, as shown in the margin illustration. Then have the child get up so you can connect the "wings" and "robe" as shown.

As you trace children, tell them that God sent an angel named Gabriel to Mary and that the angel told Mary that Jesus is God's special gift. Help children tape up their angels around the room.

The Point

> ✔ If you have an adult or teenage helper, have that person cut out children's angels.

Option 2: Mary and Joseph Living Center (up to 10 minutes)

Set up an area in your room where children can pretend to be Mary and Joseph. Set out dress-up clothing such as robes, towels, belts or pieces of string, and scarves. You might also include kitchen and household items such as pretend food, dishes, and a broom. If you have toy tools in your classroom, set them out along with wooden blocks so children can pretend to be carpenters like Joseph.

Explain that angels appeared to Mary and Joseph to tell them about baby Jesus' coming. As the children play, talk about what Mary and Joseph each might have been doing when the angels appeared. Have children act out the things they mention.

☐ **OPTION 3: Surprise Paintings (up to 10 minutes)**

Before class, dilute one or two colors of tempera paint with water.

Set out white crayons and white sheets of paper. Have each child scribble color a design on a sheet of the white paper with a white crayon. For best results, encourage children to press hard as they color.

Hold up a child's paper. Point out that the design doesn't show up very well. Tell children that when they paint their papers, they'll get a surprise—the paint will help their designs "appear." Help children paint their papers with the paint wash. As children's designs begin appearing, tell them Mary was surprised to see an angel, just as they're surprised to see their designs. Remind

✏ The Point

children that ●the angel told Mary that Jesus is God's special gift.

> ✔ White Crayola brand crayons work well for this activity.
>
> ✔ For extra fun, let children sprinkle salt on their papers while the paint is still wet. Set aside to dry. Before sending children's artwork home, shake off the excess salt.

When everyone has arrived and you're ready to move on to Bible-Story Time, encourage the children to finish what they're doing and get ready to clean up.

Pick-Up Song

Now It's Time (up to 5 minutes)

Lead children in singing "Now It's Time" with the *cassette tape*, to the tune of "The Mulberry Bush." Encourage children to sing along as they help clean up the room.

You'll be using this song each week to alert children to start picking up. At first, they may need a little encouragement. But after a few weeks, picking up and singing along will become a familiar routine.

Sing

Now it's time to clean up our room,
Clean up our room,
Clean up our room.
Now it's time to clean up our room
And put our things away.

Will you help me? Yes, I will.
Yes, I will.
Yes, I will!
Will you help me? Yes, I will.
I'll help you right away.

(Repeat)

Jesus is God's special gift.

Bible-Story Time

Setting the Stage (up to 8 minutes)

Before class, remove the *cotton padding* from the *gift box* in the Learning Lab and set it aside for use in Lesson 3. Place a bottle of glitter glue in the *gift box*. If glitter glue won't fit in the box, put a glitter design on an index card and put the index card in the box. You can hold up the glitter glue after you show children the index card. Put the lid on the *gift box* and attach the *gift bow*. Each time you use the *gift box* make sure the *gift bow* is attached.

Tell the children you'll clap three times to get their attention. Explain that when you clap three times, they're to stop what they're doing and clap three times back. Practice this signal a few times. Encourage children to respond quickly so you'll have time for all the fun activities you've planned.

Have the children sit on the floor. Ask:

● **What did you make or do when you came to our class today?** (Made an angel shape; dressed up like Mary; painted a surprise picture.)

Say: **If you made an angel when you came to class today, move your arms like wings and pretend to fly over to your angel shape.** When children are standing by their angel shapes say: **Those are wonderful angels. Fly back to us now and sit down. If you dressed up like Mary or Joseph, stand up, take a bow, and sit down. If you painted a surprise picture, stand up, spin around, and sit down.**

Bring out the *gift box* with the bottle of glitter glue inside it. Hold the box up and ask: **Look at this pretty gift. There's a surprise inside that has something to do with our Bible story. Let's open it and see what our surprise is.**

Ask a child to open the box and hand you the bottle of glitter glue. Hold it up and ask:

● **What could this glitter glue have to do with our Bible story?** (There's an angel in our story; the glitter is shiny like an angel.)

Say: **This glitter reminds me of shining angels. Our story today is about an angel named Gabriel.** ● **Gabriel told Mary that Jesus is God's special gift. We're going to use this glitter glue in a little while to help us learn about that Bible story.**

Set the glitter glue aside and say: **Mary was surprised by the angel's visit. The Bible tells us that an angel appeared to Joseph in a dream, too, and told him about Jesus. We're going to play a surprise game now to see what that might have been like.**

I'll choose one person to be Mary or Joseph and one person to be an angel. The angel will say, "Jesus is God's special gift." Then Mary or Joseph will get to guess—without looking—who the surprise angel was. You'll each get a chance to be Mary or Joseph and the angel.

Let's practice the angel's message together first. Say with me, "Jesus is God's special gift."

Repeat the message a few times, then choose a child to be Mary or Joseph. Have the child close his or her eyes and face away from the rest of the group. Choose another child to be an angel. Have the angel stand near the first child and say, "Jesus is God's special gift." Have the child who is Mary or Joseph guess which child is speaking. Then invite the child to turn around and see who the surprise angel is. Ask:

● **The Point**

● **Are you surprised that the angel was** (name of child)**?**
Say: **Mary was surprised when the angel Gabriel came to her.**

Invite the angel to be Mary or Joseph, then choose a new angel. Continue playing until everyone has had a chance to be Mary or Joseph. Then lead the children to the story area and have them sit down.

✔ If it's too difficult for some of the children to say, "Jesus is God's special gift," shorten it to "Jesus is God's gift."

✔ If you have a large class, choose a Mary and a Joseph each time. Let Mary and Joseph take turns guessing the angel's identity before you reveal it.

Bible Song and Prayer Time (up to 5 minutes)

Say: **Each week when we come to our circle for our Bible story, I'll choose someone to be the Bible person. The Bible person will bring me the Bible marked with our Bible story for that week. Before I choose today's Bible person, let's learn our Bible song. As we sing, we'll pass around our special Bible. The person who's holding the Bible when the music stops will be our Bible person today.**

Lead children in singing "We Are Glad to Read the Bible" with the *cassette tape,* to the tune of "Did You Ever See a Lassie?" As you sing, pass around the special Bible.

Sing

We are glad to read the Bible,
The Bible, the Bible.
We are glad to read the Bible
For it is God's Book.

We'll hear Bible stories
And learn about God's love.
We are glad to read the Bible
For it is God's Book.

When the music stops, invite the child who's holding the Bible to bring it to you. Stamp the child's hand with the *angel stamp* and thank the child for bringing you the Bible. Then stamp the other children's hands. Return the *angel stamp and ink pad* to the Learning Lab.

Say: **I'm thankful for** (name of child who brought the Bible) **and I'm thankful for everyone in our class today. Let's thank God together for all our friends in this class.**

Lead children in singing "We Are Glad to Pray Together" with the *cassette tape,* to the tune of "Did You Ever See a Lassie?" If you want to include the names of all the children in your class, sing the song without the cassette and repeat the naming section. If you choose to use the cassette, vary the names you use each week.

Sing

We are glad to pray together,
Together, together.
We are glad to pray together
And give thanks to God.

Lead children in folding their
hands and bowing their heads as
you continue to sing.

Thank you for (name),
And (name), and (name).
Thank you, God, for every person
Who's here in our class.

(Repeat)

✔ Choose a special Bible to use for this section of the lesson each week. For example, you could use a big, black Bible; a red Bible; or a Bible with gold leaf pages. These special characteristics will make Bible time memorable for the children.

Hear the Bible Story (up to 5 minutes)

Before class, fold the *Learning Mat: Jesus' Birth* in thirds so only the segment with Mary and the angel, and Mary and Joseph traveling is showing. Lay the *Learning Mat* on the floor so all the children can see it. If you have a large class, you may want to tape the mat to a wall or bulletin board. Have the children gather around the mat. Ask:

● **What do you notice about this *Learning Mat* that's different from other *Learning Mats* we've had?** (There's no color; it's black and white.)

Say: **This *Learning Mat* is black and white so we can work together on making it colorful!**

Open your Bible to Luke 1 and show it to the children. Say: **Our Bible story comes from the book of Luke in the Bible. Our *Learning Mat* shows us pictures of our Bible story. I'm going to tell you about a surprise Mary received one day. Can you find Mary on our *Learning Mat?***

Help children find the picture of Mary, then continue: **Mary listened to the angel's message from God and promised to do what God wanted her to do. Whenever you hear me say "Mary," fold your hands in front of you and nod your head up and down like you're saying "yes." Let's practice that together. Mary.**

Let children practice their actions, then continue: **Mary was surprised to see an angel. But the angel told her not to be afraid. Whenever you hear me say the word "angel," I want you to say, "Don't be afraid." Let's practice that together. Angel.**

Let children practice and then tell the story using the text printed below.

One day God gave one of his <u>angels</u> a special job. The <u>angel's</u> name was Gabriel. God sent Gabriel to a town called Nazareth. Can you say Nazareth? Pause. **He went to see a woman named <u>Mary</u>. <u>Mary</u> loved God. She was getting ready to marry a man named Joseph.**

The day the <u>angel</u> came, <u>Mary</u> was working around the house. She was doing all the things she usually did. She didn't know yet that it was

a special day. As she worked, something wonderful happened! The __angel__ Gabriel came to her! He said, "Greetings! The Lord has blessed you and is with you." __Mary__ was so surprised! Show me how you look when you're surprised.

Let children show you their surprised looks then continue: **Wow! You look very surprised. Well, __Mary__ was surprised, too. She'd never seen an __angel__ before, and she didn't know why the __angel__ had come to see her.**

Then the __angel__ said, "Don't be afraid, __Mary__. You are going to have a baby. You will name him Jesus."

__Mary__ said, "How can I have a baby? I'm not married yet."

"God will help you," said the __angel__. "Your baby will be called the Son of God. God can do anything!"

__Mary__ said, "I love God. I will do everything he says."

Then the __angel__ went away.

Say: **You did the motions so well! You were good listeners!** Ask:

● **What did the angel tell Mary?** (That she would have a baby; that baby Jesus was coming; God wanted her to be Jesus' mom.)

● **How do you think Mary felt when the angel came to her?** (Surprised; scared; happy.)

● **Tell me about a time when someone surprised you.** (My mom told me she was going to have a baby; my parents told me we were going to move; my dad brought me a surprise when he came home from a trip.)

⬤ The Point

Say: **The angel told Mary that Jesus is God's special gift. When Mary heard the angel's message, she was surprised and a little scared at first. But the angel promised that God would help her. Sometimes we may get surprises that seem a little scary at first. If your mom is having a new baby, you may be scared about sharing your room or your toys. If you're moving to a new house, you may be scared about finding new friends to play with. But God will help you, just as he helped Mary. Let's decorate our *Learning Mat* picture of Mary and the angel now.**

Do the Bible Story (up to 8 minutes)

Cue the *cassette tape* to the "Angel Music" segment. Point to the picture of the angel on the *Learning Mat*. Say: **In a few moments, we're going to work on coloring the angel on our *Learning Mat* together. But first I'm going to play some heavenly music from our *cassette tape* for you. I call it heavenly because it's so pretty. The instrument you'll hear is called a harp.**

⬤ The Point

Say: **When you hear the music, let's stretch our angel wings and bodies and float around the room pretending to be angels. When the music stops, you stop. Then we'll say together, ⬤ "Jesus is God's special gift."**

Do this several times. Then say: **Now let's float back over to the story area and work on our mat. We can listen to the pretty music while we color our angel scene. When we're finished, we'll put some glitter glue on our angel's gown to make it shiny.**

Rewind the tape if necessary and continue playing the harp music while the children work. Pass out crayons and markers to each child. Let the children take turns coloring parts of the angel scene. Be sure to color only the section of the *Learning Mat* with the angel in it. Tell children that they'll get to decorate other sections of the mat during future lessons. As the children work, remind them that the angel told Mary that Jesus is God's special gift.

● **The Point**

When children have colored the angel scene to their satisfaction, let them take turns putting dots of glitter glue on the angel's gown. Have children gather around the mat to admire their work. Then set the mat aside to dry.

> ✔ If your class is large, form two or three groups. Have one group begin coloring while the others float around the room to the harp music. Have groups switch every minute or two.
>
> ✔ If you're sharing your *Learning Mat* with another class, color only a portion of it and explain that other children will finish coloring the angel picture later. One group of children can put silver or gold glitter glue on the angel, and the other group can put red or blue glitter glue on Mary's dress.

Practicing The Point

Surprise! (up to 5 minutes)

Bring out Whiskers the Mouse and go through the following puppet script. When you finish the script, put Whiskers away and out of sight.

Surprise!

PUPPET SCRIPT

Whiskers: *(Hides behind teacher, then suddenly pops out.)* Surprise! I'm here!

Teacher: Hi, Whiskers. You surprised me! I didn't hear you coming.

Whiskers: Oh, goody. I like to surprise people! I want to do it again. Close your eyes, and I'll appear somewhere else.

Teacher: Children, Whiskers wants to surprise us again. Let's close our eyes and see where he'll appear next.
(Have children close their eyes, then take Whiskers to another area of the room. Let children open their eyes, then have Whiskers pop out again.)

Whiskers: Boo! Surprise, surprise! Oh, that's so much fun. I could go on surprising you all day.

Teacher: Whiskers, all your surprises remind me of our Bible story today.

Whiskers: Oh, really? Was there a surprise in it?

(Continued)

Teacher: Yes, there was. Someone got a great surprise!

Whiskers: Oh, tell me, tell me! I love good stories! And I love surprises!

Teacher: Let's ask your friends if they can tell you about the surprise Mary got.

(Help children tell Whiskers how the angel surprised Mary with the message that she was going to be Jesus' mother.)

Whiskers: Wow! That's a great story! But if I were Mary, I would have been a little scared when the angel came. (Asks a child.) Would you have been scared? (Lets child respond then asks another child.) How about you? (Lets child respond.)

Teacher: Mary probably was a little scared at first. But the angel told Mary that Jesus is God's special gift. That made her glad! She was happy because she was going to be the mother of Jesus!

Whiskers: Well, I'm glad Mary said yes to God. She was brave! Thanks for telling me that great story. I've gotta go now! I think I'll go home and surprise my brother. Then I'll tell him the story about Mary's surprise. Bye!

 **The Point**

TODAY I LEARNED . . .

We believe Christian education extends beyond the classroom into the home. Photocopy the "Today I Learned . . ." handout (p. 31) for this week and send it home with your children. Encourage parents to use the handout to plan meaningful family activities to reinforce this week's topic. Follow up the "Today I Learned . . ." activities next week by asking children what their families did.

Closing

Jesus Is God's Gift (up to 5 minutes)

 **The Point**

Have children sit with you in a circle on the floor. Say: **The angel told Mary that Jesus is God's special gift. He's our special gift, too. Let's give each other angel stamps to help us remember that.**

Have children take turns pressing the *angel stamp* on the *ink pad* and then stamping the hand of the child sitting next to them. Each time a hand gets stamped, have everyone say together, "Jesus is God's special gift."

When everyone's been stamped, return the *angel stamp and ink pad* to the Learning Lab. Say: **Let's tell God thank you for his special gift. Dear God, thank you so much for sending us Jesus. He's our special gift.**

Give children the opportunity to pray aloud if they'd like to.

Jesus is God's special gift.

For Extra Time

If you have a long class time or want to add additional elements to your lesson, try one of the following activities.

LIVELY LEARNING: God's Gift—Jesus!

Have children sit in a circle on the floor. Designate one child as the angel. Have the angel walk around the outside of the circle and tap each child on the shoulder. As the angel taps children on the shoulder, have the angel say, "God's gift." After saying "God's gift" to several children, the angel should tap a child and say "Jesus!" Tell children that when the angel says "Jesus," they should all jump up, hug the person next to them, and then sit down. After everyone's been hugged, have the child who was tapped on "Jesus" become the next angel. Repeat the game as time allows.

MAKE TO TAKE: Angel Wrapping Paper

Set out crayons or markers and give each child a sheet of newsprint. Pass around the *angel stamp and ink pad* and let children take turns stamping angels on their newsprint. Encourage them to color the newsprint as they wait for a turn with the *angel stamp*. Explain to children that they can use the angel wrapping paper to wrap a special Christmas gift for a friend or family member. Remind them that 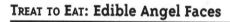 the angel told Mary that Jesus is God's special gift.

If this is your second year using Hands-On Bible Curriculum for Preschool, you may want to set out additional stamps and ink pads for children to use. Other stamps that would tie in well with Jesus' birth include the sheep stamp from Fall 1994, the manger and shepherd stamps from Winter 1994-95, and the star stamp from Fall 1995.

● The Point

TREAT TO EAT: Edible Angel Faces

Cut round paper doilies in half and set them on paper plates. You'll need a paper plate and doily half for each child.

Give each child a paper plate and doily half for the angel's collar. Help each child place a round slice of pineapple on top of the doily for the angel's head. Set out items children can use to make the angel's face and hair. Use things such as raisins or grapes for eyes and noses, cinnamon candies for mouths, and whipped cream sprinkled with coconut for hair.

STORY PICTURE: The Angel's Surprise

Give each child a copy of the "Today I Learned..." handout (p. 31). Set out glue, crayons or markers, and several colors of glitter glue. After children color their pictures, let them choose objects to decorate with glitter glue, such as the angel or Mary's clothes. As children work, review the details of today's Bible story. Remind children that ● the angel told Mary that Jesus is God's special gift.

● The Point

Jesus is God's special gift.

Angel Name Tags

Photocopy and cut out the name tags.

Permission to photocopy this handout from Group's Hands-On Bible Curriculum™ for Preschool granted for local church use.
Copyright © Group Publishing, Inc., Box 481, Loveland, CO 80539.

Jesus is God's special gift.

Permission to photocopy this handout from Group's Hands-On Bible Curriculum™ for Preschool granted for local church use. Copyright © Group Publishing, Inc., Box 481, Loveland, CO 80539.

TODAY I LEARNED . . .

The Point ✏ The angel told Mary that Jesus is God's special gift.

Today your child learned that the angel told Mary that Jesus is God's special gift. Children played a game where they surprised each other and talked about how Mary was surprised by the angel.

LESSON 1

Verse to Learn

"My heart rejoices in God my Savior" (Luke 1:47).

Ask Me . . .

● What did the angel tell Mary?

● Tell me about a time when you were surprised about something.

● What can our family do to surprise others and make them happy?

Family Fun

● Cut a Christmas card or a magazine picture into several pieces. Mix the pieces up and let your child experience the surprise of discovering the picture as he or she puts the pieces together. Talk about things you can do together this Christmas to surprise others and make them happy.

The Angel Gabriel Comes to Mary (Luke 1:26-38)

The Most Special Gift

The Point

✏ Jesus is God's special gift.

The Bible Basis

Luke 2:1-7. Jesus is born.

Mary and Joseph willingly embraced God's amazing plan for their lives. In faith and obedience, they set out for Bethlehem to register for the census—despite the fact that the birth of Mary's baby was imminent. The angels' words of promise must have sustained them through the dangers and discomforts of the journey. When they finally reached Bethlehem, they found no refuge but a smelly stable where Mary gave birth to Jesus, God's gift to the world.

Three- and 4-year-olds are filled with excitement at Christmastime. Special presents appear under Christmas trees, special songs are sung, special people come to visit. In the midst of holiday preparations and activity, preschoolers need to be reminded often of the true meaning of Christmas. Use this lesson to remind children that the most special thing about Christmas is the birth of God's Son, Jesus.

Getting The Point

✏ **Jesus is God's special gift.**

It's important to say The Point just as it's written in each activity. Repeating The Point over and over will help the children remember it and apply it to their lives.

Children will
● see how Jesus' birthplace was different from where babies are born today,
● count and take a "census" in the classroom,
● hear how Mary and Joseph traveled to Bethlehem, and
● thank God for sending Jesus.

✏ **The Point**

This Lesson at a Glance

Before the lesson, collect the necessary items for the activities you plan to use. Refer to the Classroom Supplies and Learning Lab Supplies columns to determine what you'll need. Remember to make photocopies of the "Today I Learned..." handout (p. 44) to send home with your children.

Section	Minutes	What Children Will Do	Classroom Supplies	Learning Lab Supplies
Welcome Time	up to 5	**Welcome!**—Receive name tags and be greeted by the teacher.	"Angel Name Tags" handouts (p. 30)	
Let's Get Started Direct children to one or more of the Let's Get Started activities until everyone arrives.	up to 10	**Option 1: Classroom Register**—Take a classroom "census" and hear how Mary and Joseph traveled to Bethlehem to be counted.	Newsprint, pencils, markers	
	up to 10	**Option 2: Away in a Manger**—Compare Jesus' birthplace to where babies are born today.	Baby blanket, diaper, hay, box, doll, strips of cloth	
	up to 10	**Option 3: Animals in the Stable**—Set up a pretend stable and hear how Jesus was born in a stable.	Blanket, table, stuffed animals	
Pick-Up Song	up to 5	**Now It's Time**—Sing a song as they pick up toys and gather for Bible-Story Time.	Cassette player	Cassette: "Now It's Time"
Bible-Story Time	up to 8	**Setting the Stage**—Praise baby Jesus with animal sounds.	Cassette player	Hay, gift box, cassette: "Animal Sounds," "Away in a Manger"
	up to 5	**Bible Song and Prayer Time**—Sing a song, bring out the Bible, and pray together.	Bible, cassette player	Angel stamp and ink pad, cassette: "We Are Glad ..."
	up to 10	**Hear the Bible Story**—Hear Joseph's story about traveling to Bethlehem.	Bible, crayons, markers, glue, fabric scraps	Learning Mat: Jesus' Birth, hay
	up to 5	**Do the Bible Story**—Pack for a pretend trip to Bethlehem.		
Practicing The Point	up to 5	**No Room**—Help Whiskers get over being mad that "his" room at Cousin Joey's house will be taken over by a new baby.	Whiskers the Mouse	
Closing	up to 5	**Passing Prayers**—Pass around a wrapped doll and thank God for sending Jesus.	Wrapped doll from Let's Get Started	
For Extra Time		For extra-time ideas and supplies, see page 43.		

Jesus is God's special gift.

Welcome Time

Welcome! (up to 5 minutes)

- Bend down and make eye contact with children as they arrive.
- Greet each child individually with an enthusiastic smile.
- Thank each child for coming to class today.
- As children arrive, ask them about last week's "Today I Learned..." discussion. Use questions such as "What did you tell your family about Mary's surprise?" or "How did your family surprise each other this week?"
- Say: **Today we're going to learn that** 🖊 **Jesus is God's special gift.**
- Hand out the angel name tags children made during Lesson 1 and help them attach the name tags to their clothing. If some of the name tags were damaged or if children weren't in class that week, have them make new name tags using the photocopiable handout on page 30.
- Direct children to the Let's Get Started activities you've set up.

✏ **The Point**

Let's Get Started

Set up one or more of the following activities for children to do as they arrive. After you greet each child, invite him or her to choose an activity.

Circulate among the children to offer help as needed and direct children's conversation toward the point of today's lesson. Ask questions such as "Tell me about the best Christmas present you ever got" or "What would it be like to be born in a barn?"

▢ OPTION 1: Classroom Register (up to 10 minutes)

Set a sheet of newsprint on a table or work area. Set out markers or crayons and let children "sign" their names on the paper. Some children may be able to write their own names; others may need adult help. Encourage children to "write" or scribble their own names unless they ask for help. Or invite them to create a hand print "signature" by tracing around their hands.

Stop occasionally and have children help you count the signatures on your newsprint. Encourage everyone to sign the "register." If you wish, count the children in the class and see if the number of children matches the number of signatures on the paper.

As children work, talk about how Mary and Joseph traveled to Bethlehem to be counted. They had to sign their names, and when all the names were counted, the government knew how many people there were. Explain that Jesus was born while Mary and Joseph were in Bethlehem. Remind children that ● Jesus is God's special gift.

● **The Point**

▢ OPTION 2: Away in a Manger (up to 10 minutes)

Before class, borrow a blanket and diaper from your church's nursery. You'll also need hay or shredded newspaper, a medium-sized box, a doll, and strips of cloth (enough to wrap the doll).

Hold up the diaper and the blanket and explain that we take care of babies today by making sure they have dry diapers and by wrapping them in warm blankets. Tell children that the Bible says Jesus was wrapped in strips of cloth. Use the strips of cloth and the doll to demonstrate how Mary and Joseph might have wrapped up baby Jesus. Let the children try wrapping up the doll.

Then show children the box and the hay. Invite them to tell you what kinds of beds babies sleep in today and then explain that baby Jesus slept in a manger—an animal feeding box.

When children have all had a turn to wrap the doll and lay it gently in the manger bed, have children sit in a circle as you sing "Away in a Manger" together.

Sing

Away in a manger,
No crib for a bed,
The little Lord Jesus
Laid down his sweet head.

The stars in the sky
Looked down where he lay.
The little Lord Jesus
Asleep on the hay.

(Repeat)

☐ OPTION 3: Animals in the Stable (up to 10 minutes)

Invite children to help you make a pretend stable by putting a blanket over a classroom table or chairs. Bring in a variety of stuffed animals and talk about what animals might have been in the stable when Jesus was born. Discuss what would be good about having animals in the place where a baby would be born. Then talk about what would be bad about that. Let children play with the animals in the stable you've set up. Encourage them to take turns being Mary, Joseph, and baby Jesus. As they play, remind them that Christmas is the time we celebrate Jesus' birth, and that 🖊 Jesus is God's special gift.

🖊 The Point

When everyone has arrived and you're ready to move on to Bible-Story Time, encourage the children to finish what they're doing and get ready to clean up.

Pick-Up Song

Now It's Time (up to 5 minutes)

Lead children in singing "Now It's Time" with the *cassette tape*, to the tune of "The Mulberry Bush." Encourage children to sing along as they help clean up the room.

Sing

Now it's time to clean up our room,
Clean up our room,
Clean up our room.
Now it's time to clean up our room
And put our things away.

Will you help me? Yes, I will.
Yes, I will.
Yes, I will!
Will you help me? Yes, I will.
I'll help you right away.

(Repeat)

Jesus is God's special gift.

Bible-Story Time

Setting the Stage (up to 8 minutes)

Before class, put the *hay* from the Learning Lab inside the *gift box*. Set the manger box from Let's Get Started in the story area. If you didn't bring a box, set out a chair to represent the manger. Have the *cassette tape* cued to play the "Animal Sounds" segment.

Tell children you'll clap three times to get their attention. Explain that when you clap three times, the children are to stop what they're doing and repeat the clap. Practice this signal a few times. Encourage children to respond quickly so you'll have time for all the fun activities you've planned.

Gather the children in an area other than your story area and ask:

● **What did you make or do when you came to our class today?** (Signed my name on the paper; wrapped up baby Jesus; played in a pretend stable.)

Say: **Some of you signed your names on our class register. Some of you learned about the different clothes and bed baby Jesus had. And some of you played in our pretend stable. You were all learning important things about our Bible story. If you signed your name on our classroom register, clap your hands and count to five with me.**

Clap your hands and count to five with the children, then continue: **If you wrapped up a doll in pieces of cloth and put him in our manger box, raise both hands in the air then put them down.** Pause. **If you played in the stable with the animals, moo like a cow, then be quiet as a mouse.**

Bring out the *gift box* with the *hay* inside. Hold the box up and ask: **Look at this pretty gift box. There's something inside this box that has to do with our Bible story. Let's open it and see what it is.**

Ask a child to open the box and hand you the *hay.* Hold it up and ask:

● **What could this *hay* have to do with our Bible story?** (Jesus slept in a manger with hay in it; there was hay in the stable.)

This *hay* reminds me of the stable where Jesus was born. That's what our Bible story is about. Today we'll be learning that ⬢ Jesus is God's special gift, and we'll hear how he was born in Bethlehem. We're going to use this *hay* in a little while when we're finished hearing our story.

Set the *hay* aside and ask:

● **Who likes to eat hay?** (Animals; cows; not me.)

● **What animals do you think were in the stable where Jesus was born?** (Cows; sheep; donkeys.)

● **What do you think it was like in the stable with all those animals?** (Noisy; stinky; fun.)

Say: **Let's pretend to be animals and go to the stable. We can praise Jesus with our animal noises when we get there. Think of an animal you want to be.**

Lead children to the stable from Let's Get Started (or another designated area), then invite them to tell you what animals they've chosen. Then say: **Let's all pretend to be the animals we've chosen. I'm going to play some animal sounds on it. Let's join those animals and make our own animal sounds. We can pretend to welcome baby Jesus.**

Play the "Animal Sounds" segment from the *cassette tape.* As you listen to the sounds, lead children in crawling around the room like animals. Circle around the room a few times, then stop, arriving at your story area.

● **The Point**

● The Point

When everyone has arrived, stop the tape and say together: ●**Jesus is God's special gift.**

Say: **It was fun to pretend to welcome baby Jesus with animal sounds. Now let's praise Jesus with people sounds by singing a song to worship Jesus and tell him we love him.**

Lead the children in singing "Away in a Manger" with the *cassette tape.* "Away in a Manger" is recorded on the cassette twice. If children don't know the song, have them listen the first time, then sing along.

Sing

Away in a manger,
No crib for a bed,
The little Lord Jesus
Laid down his sweet head.

The stars in the sky
Looked down where he lay.
The little Lord Jesus
Asleep on the hay.

(Repeat)

Bible Song and Prayer Time (up to 5 minutes)

Say: **Now it's time to choose a Bible person to bring me the Bible marked with today's Bible story. As we sing our Bible song, we'll pass around our special Bible. The person who's holding the Bible when the music stops will be our Bible person today.**

Lead children in singing "We Are Glad to Read the Bible" with the *cassette tape,* to the tune of "Did You Ever See a Lassie?" As you sing, pass around the special Bible.

Sing

We are glad to read the Bible,
The Bible, the Bible.
We are glad to read the Bible
For it is God's Book.

We'll hear Bible stories
And learn about God's love.
We are glad to read the Bible
For it is God's Book.

When the music stops, invite the child who's holding the Bible to bring it to you. Stamp the child's hand with the *angel stamp* and thank the child for bringing you the Bible. Then stamp the other children's hands. Return the *angel stamp and ink pad* to the Learning Lab.

Say: **I'm thankful for** (name of child who brought the Bible) **and I'm thankful for everyone in our class today. Let's thank God together for all our friends in this class.**

Lead children in singing "We Are Glad to Pray Together" with the *cassette tape,* to the tune of "Did You Ever See a Lassie?" If you want to include the names of all the children in your class, sing the song without the cassette and repeat the naming section. If you choose to use the cassette, vary the names you use each week.

Jesus is God's special gift.

Sing

We are glad to pray together,
Together, together.
We are glad to pray together
And give thanks to God.

Lead children in folding their
hands and bowing their heads as
you continue to sing.

Thank you for (name),
And (name), **and** (name).
Thank you, God, for every person
Who's here in our class.

(Repeat)

Hear the Bible Story (up to 10 minutes)

Before class, fold the *Learning Mat* so that only the first panel is showing. Hang the *Learning Mat* on a wall near your story area.

Open your Bible to Luke 2 and show it to the children. Say: **Our Bible story comes from the book of Luke in the Bible. Our *Learning Mat* shows us pictures of our Bible story.**

Point to the picture of the angel that children decorated last week. Ask:
● **Who is this with the sparkling clothes?** (An angel.)
● **What is the angel doing?** (Talking to Mary; he told Mary she was going to be Jesus' mother.)

Say: **Last week we learned about the angel that told Mary that Jesus would be born. This week we're going to pretend we're Joseph and hear how Joseph and Mary traveled to Bethlehem. Can you find Mary and Joseph on our *Learning Mat?***

Let children point out the picture of Mary and Joseph traveling. Then say: **Let's all stand up while we hear their story. I'll say and do something, then you say and do it after me.**

I'm Joseph. *(Point to self.)*
My wife, Mary, is going to be Jesus' mother. *(Pretend to cradle a baby.)*
That makes me happy! *(Smile.)*
But first we have to travel far, far away. *(Point thumb over shoulder.)*
C'mon, it's time to go! *(Make a beckoning motion.)*
We walk and walk and walk. *(Walk in place.)*
It's a long way to Bethlehem! *(Nod head.)*
Finally we're there! Phew! *(Wipe hand across forehead.)*
We need a place to sleep. *(Put hand above eyes, searching.)*
So I knock on the door of an inn. *(Make knocking motion.)*
"No room!" shouts the owner. *(Cup hands around mouth.)*
So I knock on another door. *(Make knocking motion.)*
"Full up!" yells the innkeeper. *(Cup hands around mouth.)*
"But the baby..." I say. *(Cradle arms.)*
"Did you say 'baby'?" *(Point finger toward someone.)*
"Yes, my wife, Mary, is about to have a baby." *(Cradle arms.)*
"Come this way," he says. *(Beckon with hand toward self.)*

Open the *Learning Mat* so children can see the picture of the stable on the second panel, then continue.

He takes us to a stable. *(Walk in place.)*
It's warm and dry. *(Wrap arms around self.)*
We can rest here for the night. *(Lay head on hands.)*

Jesus is God's special gift.

Late in the night, I hear a baby cry! *(Cup hand over ear as if listening.)*
It's Jesus! He's here! *(Spread arms out wide.)*
We're so happy! *(Jump up and down.)*
Mary wraps Jesus in pieces of cloth. *(Make wrapping motions.)*
She lays him in a box where animals eat. *(Pretend to lay baby down.)*
It's OK that we don't have a real bed! *(Nod head.)*
Jesus is here! *(Spread arms out wide.)*
That's what matters! *(Nod head.)*
Jesus is God's special gift! *(Clap.)*

Have children sit down. Ask:

● **Where was Jesus born?** (In a stable; where animals live; in Bethlehem.)

● **How do you think Mary and Joseph felt about having their baby born in a stable?** (They were happy Jesus was going to be born; worried; scared.)

● The Point

Say: **Mary and Joseph trusted God. They were happy that Jesus was going to be born. They knew that ✎ Jesus is God's special gift. That was the most important thing of all.**

Gently take down the *Learning Mat* and set it on the floor or on a table. Give children crayons or markers to color the picture of Mary and Joseph traveling to Bethlehem. Then bring out the *hay* from the *gift box* you opened during Setting the Stage. Help children spread glue on the manger and stable floor and glue down bits of *hay*. If you wish, have a piece of fabric available to glue on baby Jesus as swaddling clothes.

When children finish decorating the stable scene, let them color it. Fold the mat so panels one and two are showing, then put it back on the wall. Congratulate children for their good work, then invite them to join you in the story area.

Do the Bible Story (up to 5 minutes)

Ask:

● **If you were Mary and Joseph and you were getting ready to go to Bethlehem, what are some things you'd be sure to take with you?** (Food; clothes for themselves and Jesus; toothbrush; blankets.)

Have children spread out around the room. Say: **I'm ready to go to Bethlehem. You can join me when you get tapped on the shoulder. When someone taps you, tell us what you want to take on the trip.**

Move among the children and say: **I'm going to Bethlehem and I'm taking a donkey.** Tap a child on the shoulder and ask: **What will you take?**

Have that child name an item such as a toy, a snack, or pajamas.

Join hands together and move around the room. Say together: **We're going on a trip to Bethlehem. We're taking a donkey and a** (have the child repeat his or her item)**.** Then have that child tap another child on the shoulder. Ask the second child: **What will you take?**

Have that child name an item and join hands with you.

Repeat the words and actions until you've tapped everyone. Have children each name their items one more time, then travel over to your story area ("Bethlehem") and sit down.

Say: **Bethlehem was a long way from where Mary and Joseph lived. They had to pack enough clothes and food for several days. When they got to Bethlehem, they couldn't find any place to stay, so they had to** stay in a stable. That's where Jesus was born. ✏️ Jesus is God's special gift. Let's tell our friend Whiskers about Jesus' birth in Bethlehem.

Practicing The Point

No Room (up to 5 minutes)

Bring out Whiskers the Mouse and go through the following puppet script. When you finish the script, put Whiskers away and out of sight.

No Room

PUPPET SCRIPT

Whiskers: *(Arms crossed, head hanging)* Humph! I'm so mad!

Teacher: What's wrong, Whiskers?

Whiskers: Oh, hi. *(Pouting)* I just got home from Cousin Joey's house. I'm not spending the night there anymore!

Teacher: Why not?

Whiskers: Well, I was supposed to stay with Cousin Joey's family while my parents were out of town.

Teacher: That sounds like fun. You like playing with Cousin Joey.

Whiskers: Yeah, but when I got to Joey's house the playroom we always sleep in was gone!

Teacher: What do you mean it was gone?

Whiskers: I went to put my sleeping bag where I always put it, but there was a crib in the way! And a bunch of diapers and blankets and baby toys. Cousin Joey said we couldn't sleep in there anymore. And we couldn't play with any of the toys either.

Teacher: Whiskers, it sounds like Cousin Joey's family is going to have a new baby! That's exciting!

Whiskers: Not to me it isn't! There wasn't any room for me and Cousin Joey to sleep in there. Now we have to sleep in his room with his brothers.

Teacher: I see. *(Pause.)* You know, Whiskers, Jesus' mother and father had trouble finding a place to sleep, too.

Whiskers: They did?

Teacher: They needed a place to stay the night Jesus was born. Children, can you tell Whiskers what happened when Mary and Joseph tried to find a place to stay in Bethlehem? *(Help children tell Whiskers how there was no room at the inn, so Mary and Joseph stayed in a stable with the animals.)*

Whiskers: Wow, that's really something . . . They slept in a

(Continued)

Jesus is God's special gift.

stable! With animals! And Jesus didn't mind being born there? Boy, they were brave!

Teacher: Mary and Joseph were grateful for a warm place where Jesus could be born. Jesus is God's special gift.

Whiskers: Well, if Jesus could share a stable with animals, I suppose I should be happy sharing a room with Joey and his brothers.

Teacher: Besides, Whiskers, you and Joey will love that new baby so much you'll be glad for him to have that room!

Whiskers: I guess you're right. Now that you mention it, I am a little excited! Baby mice are really cute! *(Pauses.)* I think I need to tell Cousin Joey I'm sorry for being mad. I'll see you later! Thanks for helping me, everybody!

● The Point

TODAY I LEARNED...

We believe Christian education extends beyond the classroom into the home. Photocopy the "Today I Learned..." handout (p. 44) for this week and send it home with your children. Encourage parents to use the handout to plan meaningful family activities to reinforce this week's topic. Follow up the "Today I Learned..." activities next week by asking children what their families did.

Closing

Passing Prayers (up to 5 minutes)

● The Point

Gather children in a circle. Say: **Mary and Joseph traveled a long way to get to Bethlehem. Do you remember why Mary and Joseph had to go to Bethlehem? They went to be counted, along with lots of other people. Let's do some counting now as we take turns thanking God for Jesus. ● Jesus is God's special gift.**

Hold up the wrapped doll you used during Let's Get Started. Say: **We'll pretend this doll is baby Jesus. As we gently pass the doll around the circle, we'll count to three. If you're holding the doll when we count "three," it will be your turn to pray, "Thank you, God, for Jesus."**

Continue counting and passing the doll until everyone has had a chance to pray. If children are shy about praying alone, repeat the prayer together.

For Extra Time

If you have a long class time or want to add additional elements to your lesson, try one of the following activities.

LIVELY LEARNING: Ride Your Donkey to Bethlehem

Have children line up on one side of the room. Stand across the room from the children, and tell them you're in "Bethlehem." Explain that each time you say, "Ride your donkey to Bethlehem," you'll give them instructions such as "Take two giant steps." Children are to follow your instructions until they reach "Bethlehem."

Use the following instructions or add additional instructions of your own.
- **Take three baby steps.**
- **Twirl one time.**
- **Jump three jumps.**
- **Hop two hops.**
- **Take one step backward.**

When children reach Bethlehem, choose a child to be the leader. Let children play the game as long as they're interested. As they play, remind them that Jesus was born in Bethlehem and that ✏️Jesus is God's special gift.

The Point

MAKE TO TAKE: Craft-Stick Manger Prints

Cover a table with newsprint and give each child a sheet of brown construction paper. Set out pans of yellow tempera paint and give each child a large craft stick. Show each child how to hold the stick and dip the long, thin edge into the paint and "print" with the stick edge onto the brown paper.

Explain that the yellow lines on the paper can be the hay in Jesus' manger. Show children how to make lines pointing in different directions. Let children continue printing until they're satisfied with the number of lines they've made.

Then set out construction paper circles for baby Jesus' face and fabric-scrap ovals for his body. Let children put Jesus in the manger by gluing the shapes on their papers. As children complete their pictures remind them that ✏️Jesus is God's special gift.

The Point

TREAT TO EAT: Chow Mein Mangers

Give each child a wax paper square, a spoonful of peanut butter, and a handful of chow mein noodles. Show children how to arrange the chow mein noodles as "hay" in the peanut butter "manger." As children create their mangers, review how Mary and Joseph laid baby Jesus in a manger. Remind them that ✏️Jesus is God's special gift.

The Point

STORY PICTURE: Jesus Is Born

Give each child a copy of the "Today I Learned..." handout (p. 44). Set out crayons or markers, glue, and small fabric scraps. After children color their pictures, let them glue one or two fabric scraps to Jesus' blanket. As they work, review the details of today's Bible story. Remind children that ✏️Jesus is God's special gift.

The Point

Jesus is God's special gift.

TODnY I LEARNED . . .

The Point ✏ Jesus is God's special gift.

Today your child learned that Jesus is God's special gift. Children compared Jesus' birthplace to where babies are born today. They heard how Jesus was born in Bethlehem and thanked God for sending Jesus.

Verse to Learn

"My heart rejoices in God my Savior" (Luke 1:47).

Ask Me . . .

● What kind of a place was Jesus born in?
● Tell me about a special gift you received.
● What special gifts can our family give to help us celebrate Jesus' birth?

Family Fun

● Bring out the family photo album and look at baby pictures of each person in your family. Talk about how surprised and happy you were when you learned that your child was going to be born. Tell your child one or two things that were special about his or her birth.

Jesus Is Born (Luke 2:1-7)

Permission to photocopy this handout from Group's Hands-On Bible Curriculum™ for Preschool granted for local church use. Copyright © Group Publishing, Inc., Box 481, Loveland, CO 80539.

Just a Shepherd

The Point

✏️ The shepherds were glad that Jesus is God's special gift.

The Bible Basis

Luke 2:8-15. Angels announce Jesus' birth to shepherds.

In Bible times, shepherds held a humble position in society. Day after day, night after night, they watched their sheep. They had little social status, wealth, or education. It would never occur to them that the God of the universe might choose them to be the first to hear of Messiah's birth. When the sky filled with angels, the shepherds were awed and amazed. After hearing the angels' message, they immediately left their sheep and hurried to find the newborn Savior.

Sometimes it's easy for young children to feel less important than adults. Three- and 4-year-olds are often told they're not big enough, fast enough, or old enough to do certain things. But like the shepherds, they are important to God. Little ones need to be reassured that they are a special part of God's plan. Use this lesson to help children discover that God's special gift, Jesus, is for them too!

Getting The Point

✏️ **The shepherds were glad that Jesus is God's special gift.**

It's important to say The Point just as it's written in each activity. Repeating The Point over and over will help the children remember it and apply it to their lives.

Children will
● dress up and act out being shepherds,
● sing a song about Jesus' birth,
● help Whiskers learn he is important to God, and
● say a prayer to thank God for sending Jesus.

⬤ **The Point**

Jesus is God's special gift.

This Lesson at a Glance

Before the lesson, collect the necessary items for the activities you plan to use. Refer to the Classroom Supplies and Learning Lab Supplies columns to determine what you'll need. Remember to make photocopies of the "Today I Learned..." handout (p. 57) to send home with your children.

Section	Minutes	What Children Will Do	Classroom Supplies	Learning Lab Supplies
Welcome Time	up to 5	**Welcome!**—Receive name tags and be greeted by the teacher.	"Angel Name Tags" handouts (p. 30)	
Let's Get Started Direct children to one or more of the Let's Get Started activities until everyone arrives.	up to 10	**Option 1: Shepherd's Corner**—Experience a day in the life of a shepherd.	Bathrobes, towels, belts or rope, yard sticks, Bible-story book, wool piece, bread, cheese	
	up to 10	**Option 2: Sheep Puppets**—Make sheep puppets and hear about the shepherds who went to see Jesus.	Old socks, glue, black marker, newsprint, cotton balls or fiberfill stuffing	
	up to 10	**Option 3: Modeling-Dough Sheep**—Make a sheepfold and talk about the shepherds who went to see Jesus.	Modeling dough	
Pick-Up Song	up to 5	**Now It's Time**—Sing a song as they pick up toys and gather for Bible-Story Time.	Cassette player	Cassette: "Now It's Time"
Bible-Story Time	up to 8	**Setting the Stage**—March and sing a song about Jesus' birth.	Yardsticks, blocks, cassette player	Gift box, gift bow, cotton padding, cassette: "Jesus Christ Is Born"
	up to 5	**Bible Song and Prayer Time**—Sing a song, bring out the Bible, and pray together.	Bible, cassette player	Angel stamp and ink pad, cassette: "We Are Glad..."
	up to 5	**Hear the Bible Story**—Pretend to be shepherds as they hear how the shepherds went to see Jesus.	Bible, fiberfill stuffing	Learning Mat: Jesus' Birth
	up to 10	**Do the Bible Story**—Play a following game and decorate the Learning Mat.	Fiberfill stuffing, crayons, markers, glue	Learning Mat, star stickers
Practicing The Point	up to 5	**Woolly Whiskers**—Tell Whiskers the story of the shepherds.	Whiskers the Mouse, fiberfill stuffing, tape	Learning Mat
Closing	up to 5	**Five Happy Shepherds**—Learn a finger play about the shepherds.	Washable markers	
For Extra Time		For extra-time ideas and supplies, see page 56.		

Jesus is God's special gift.

Welcome Time

Welcome! (up to 5 minutes)

- Bend down and make eye contact with children as they arrive.
- Greet each child individually with an enthusiastic smile.
- Thank each child for coming to class today.
- As children arrive, ask them about last week's "Today I Learned..." discussion. Use questions such as "What did you tell your family about Jesus' birth?" or "What special gifts did your family give each other?"
- Say: **Today we're going to learn that ✎ the shepherds were glad that Jesus is God's special gift.**

✎ The Point

- Hand out the angel name tags children made during Lesson 1 and help them attach the name tags to their clothing. If some of the name tags were damaged or if children weren't in class that week, have them make new name tags using the photocopiable handout on page 30.
- Direct children to the Let's Get Started activities you've set up.

Let's Get Started

Set up one or more of the following activities for children to do as they arrive. After you greet each child, invite him or her to choose an activity.

Circulate among the children to offer help as needed and direct children's conversation toward the point of today's lesson. Ask questions such as "Have you ever seen a real sheep? Tell me about it" or "What kind of things would you do if you were a shepherd?"

OPTION 1: Shepherd's Corner (up to 10 minutes)

Set up a shepherd's corner in one area of your classroom. Set out a children's Bible or Bible-story book that illustrates what shepherds in Bible times looked like. Bring in yardsticks, bathrobes, towels, and belts or rope for children to use to dress up as shepherds. Show children the pictures, then help them create their own shepherd costumes. They can tie on the towels as headdresses and use the yardsticks as shepherds' staffs.

Set out pieces of wool yarn or fabric for children to feel. Provide an unsliced loaf of bread and a chunk of cheese for children to sample. As children dress up and look at, touch, and taste the items you've set out, talk about the life of a shepherd. Explain that shepherds watched sheep all day and often took simple food such as bread and cheese along with them. Point out that ✎ the shepherds were glad that Jesus is God's special gift.

✎ The Point

✔ If you don't have bathrobes, bring in adult-sized T-shirts and tie them in the middle with a belt or piece of rope.

OPTION 2: Sheep Puppets (up to 10 minutes)

Bring in an old sock for each child in your class. Have each child choose a sock to put on his or her hand. Show children how to push the socks between their thumbs and fingers to make puppet mouths. Help children draw eyes on their puppets with a black marker. Then have children take the puppets off their hands and stuff the puppets with newsprint. Have an adult helper put glue on the back of each sock, above the eyes. Let children press fiberfill stuffing or cotton balls onto the glue. As children work on their puppets, explain that today's Bible story is about shepherds who went to find baby Jesus. Point out that ⬤ the shepherds were glad that Jesus is God's special gift.

Write children's names on their puppets and set them aside to dry. When the glue dries, remove the paper stuffing and have children put their puppets on their hands. You'll have an instant flock of little lambs!

> ✔ If you need help collecting socks, call several parents and ask them to bring in socks that have "lost their mates" or have holes in them.

OPTION 3: Modeling-Dough Sheep (up to 10 minutes)

⬤ The Point

Set out modeling dough and show children how to make dough balls to represent sheep. Have children help you make a dough fence to represent a sheepfold. Explain that a sheepfold is a safe place where shepherds put their sheep for the night to protect them from animals and robbers. Ask children to help you fill up the sheepfold with as many sheep as they can. Count the sheep together. Tell children that today's story is about the shepherds who were told where to find baby Jesus. Explain that ⬤ the shepherds were glad that Jesus is God's special gift.

When everyone has arrived and you're ready to move on to Bible-Story Time, encourage the children to finish what they're doing and get ready to clean up.

Pick-Up Song

Now It's Time (up to 5 minutes)

Lead children in singing "Now It's Time" with the *cassette tape,* to the tune of "The Mulberry Bush." Encourage children to sing along as they help clean up the room.

Sing

Now it's time to clean up our room,	Will you help me? Yes, I will.
Clean up our room,	Yes, I will.
Clean up our room.	Yes, I will!
Now it's time to clean up our room	Will you help me? Yes, I will.
And put our things away.	I'll help you right away.

(Repeat)

Bible-Story Time

Setting the Stage (up to 8 minutes)

Before class, pull apart the *cotton padding* from the *gift box* so the soft side is facing out. Put the *cotton padding* inside the *gift box*.

Tell children you'll clap three times to get their attention. Explain that when you clap three times, the children are to stop what they're doing and repeat the clap. Practice this signal a few times. Encourage children to respond quickly so you'll have time for all the fun activities you've planned.

Gather the children around you and ask:

● **What did you make or do when you came to our class today?** (Dressed up like a shepherd; made a sheep puppet; made dough sheep.)

Say: **Some of you dressed up like a shepherd. If you dressed up like a shepherd stand up and say, "I'm a shepherd," then sit down.** Pause. **Some of you made sheep puppets. If you made a sheep puppet, raise your hand and say "baa-aa!"** Pause. **Some of you made modeling-dough sheep and counted them. If you made dough sheep stand up and say, "One, two, three," then sit down.**

Bring out the *gift box* with the *cotton padding* inside. Hold the box up and ask:

● **Remember our pretty *gift box*? What did we have in it for our other lessons?** (Glitter glue; hay.)

Say: **In our other lessons, we had glitter glue to remind us of angels, and *hay* to remind us of the manger where Jesus slept. Let's open the box and see what's in it today.**

Ask a child to open the box. Have the child hand you the *cotton padding*. Hold it up and ask:

● **What could this cotton have to do with our Bible story?** (There were sheep; the shepherds saw Jesus.)

Say: **This cotton reminds me of the sheep that the shepherds were taking care of when the angel came and told them that Jesus was born. That's what our Bible story is about today.** ✏️**The shepherds were glad that Jesus is God's special gift. We're going to use this cotton after we've heard our story. Right now we're going to sing a special song to get ready for our story. First we'll listen to it, then we'll sing it together.**

Set the cotton aside. Lead children in singing "Jesus Christ Is Born" with the *cassette tape,* to the tune of "The Farmer's in the Dell." The song is recorded on

● **The Point**

the cassette twice. Encourage children to sing along with you the second time.

Sing

Jesus Christ is born!
Jesus Christ is born!
Born today in Bethlehem,
Jesus Christ is born!

Lying in a manger,
Lying in a manger,
Born today in Bethlehem,
Jesus Christ is born!

Glory to God!
Glory to God!
Born today in Bethlehem (or
   Peace on earth, good will
   toward men),
Jesus Christ is born!

(Repeat)

After the children are familiar with the song, pass out the yardsticks you used as shepherds' staffs during Let's Get Started. Give other children blocks or rhythm instruments to use while singing and marching. Rewind the tape and then have children march around the room pretending to be shepherds as they sing.

After the song, collect the staffs and instruments and have the children sit down. Ask:

● **How do you think the shepherds felt when the angel told them to go find Jesus in the stable?** (Surprised; happy; excited.)

Say: ●**The shepherds were glad that Jesus is God's special gift. And do you know what? Jesus is our special gift from God, too! Let's get ready to hear about baby Jesus and the shepherds now.**

● **The Point**

Bible Song and Prayer Time (up to 5 minutes)

Say: **Now it's time to choose a Bible person to bring me the Bible marked with today's Bible story. As we sing our Bible song, we'll pass around our special Bible. The person who's holding the Bible when the music stops will be our Bible person today.**

Lead children in singing "We Are Glad to Read the Bible" with the *cassette tape,* to the tune of "Did You Ever See a Lassie?" As you sing, pass around the special Bible.

Sing

We are glad to read the Bible,
The Bible, the Bible.
We are glad to read the Bible
For it is God's Book.

We'll hear Bible stories
And learn about God's love.
We are glad to read the Bible
For it is God's Book.

When the music stops, invite the child who's holding the Bible to bring it to you. Stamp the child's hand with the *angel stamp* and thank the child for bringing you the Bible. Then stamp the other children's hands. Return the *angel stamp and ink pad* to the Learning Lab.

Say: **I'm thankful for** (name of child who brought the Bible) **and I'm thankful for everyone in our class today. Let's thank God together for all our friends in this class.**

Lead children in singing "We Are Glad to Pray Together" with the *cassette tape,* to the tune of "Did You Ever See a Lassie?" If you want to include the

Jesus is God's special gift.

names of all the children in your class, sing the song without the cassette and repeat the naming section. If you choose to use the cassette, vary the names you use each week.

Sing

We are glad to pray together,
Together, together.
We are glad to pray together
And give thanks to God.

Lead children in folding their hands and bowing their heads as you continue to sing.

Thank you for (name),
And (name), **and** (name).
Thank you, God, for every person
Who's here in our class.

(Repeat)

Hear the Bible Story (up to 5 minutes)

Open the *Learning Mat* and fold back the panel with the three wise men. Post the folded-back *Learning Mat* on a wall in the story area. Have a bag of fiberfill stuffing on hand.

Open your Bible to Luke 2 and show it to the children. Say: **Our Bible story comes from the book of Luke in the Bible. Our *Learning Mat* shows us pictures of our Bible story.** Point to the picture of the manger that children worked on last week and ask:

● **Does anyone remember the story we heard last week? Can you tell me what happened in the stable?** (Jesus was born; Mary and Joseph and Jesus stayed there.)

Say: **Jesus was born in the stable.** Point to the manger. **You helped glue *hay* onto our *Learning Mat* manger to make it look real.**

● **Where are babies usually born today?** (In a hospital; at home; don't know.)

Say: **Today, babies are usually born in the hospital or at home with help from doctors. But God chose for Jesus to be born in a stable. That was a surprise to everyone. God had another surprise for people. Instead of telling kings or queens or important people about Jesus, God sent angels to tell the shepherds first! I want you to pretend you're a shepherd while I tell the story today. I'm going to give you each a clump of this fuzzy fiberfill stuffing. I want you to hold it during our story. You can pretend it's your sheep.**

Pass out a clump of stuffing to each child. Say: **I can see that all of you shepherds are ready with your sheep! As I tell the story, I want you to help me. Every time you hear me say the word "sheep" or "shepherd," I want you to pet your sheep and say "baa." Are you ready? Let's practice.**

Say the words "sheep" and "shepherd," then pause for children to say "baa" and pet their pretend sheep.

Then say: **That was very good. Is everyone ready for our story? Let's begin!**

It was the night that baby Jesus was born. Everything was quiet and dark in the city. People were sleeping. But out in the fields on the edge of town, some <u>shepherds</u> were quietly watching their <u>sheep</u>, just like they did every night.

Point to the sheep on the *Learning Mat* and say: **Here are the <u>sheep</u> on** our *Learning Mat* **picture. Let's count how many there are in our picture.** Count the sheep together.

Now while the sheep **ate and rested, some of the** shepherds **watched the night sky. It was filled with thousands of dancing stars shimmering down on them. What a beautiful night!**

Suddenly, a bright and shining angel appeared to the shepherds**. The** shepherds **were very afraid. Can you show me how they looked?** Pause. **The angel said to them, "Do not be afraid. I am bringing you good news that will make everyone happy. Today your Savior was born in Bethlehem. You will find him wrapped in pieces of cloth and lying in a manger."**

Then lots of other angels joined the first angel. They sang and praised God. They said, "Glory to God! Peace on earth to those who please God!" Then the angels went back to heaven.

Then everything was dark and quiet again. The shepherds **said to each other, "Let's go to Bethlehem! Let's see this thing God has told us about." So the** shepherds **said goodbye to their** sheep **and hurried to town. They found Mary and Joseph and the baby. The baby was lying in a manger, just like the angel said. The** shepherds **loved baby Jesus and knew he was the Savior. They knew he was special. So they gave thanks in their hearts to God.**  **The** shepherds **were glad that Jesus is God's special gift.**

 **The Point**

That's the end of our story today. You were good helpers. Now I'd like you to hold your sheep quietly in your laps while we talk about our story for a minute. Ask:

● **How did the shepherds feel when the angels told them about Jesus being born?** (Excited; happy; first they were scared and then glad.)

● **Did you ever feel important and special when someone told you important news? Tell us about it.** (My friend told me he got a new bike; my mom told me I was going to have a baby brother or sister.)

Say: **We feel proud and happy when people tell us important news. The shepherds didn't know they were special or important, but God thought they were! They got to be the first ones to see Jesus. They felt special!**  **The shepherds were glad that Jesus is God's special gift. And Jesus is God's special gift to you and me, too.**

 **The Point**

Do the Bible Story (up to 10 minutes)

Have children stand and hold their fiberfill sheep. Say: **We're going to play a game called Follow the Shepherd. I'll start by being the shepherd and you follow me. Take your sheep with you and do what I do. Then we'll come back here and decorate our *Learning Mat*.**

Lead children around the room. Demonstrate the actions listed below for children to imitate as they follow you.
● hopping
● twirling
● sitting down and petting their sheep
● skipping
● raising their sheep up in the air
● saying, "Jesus is God's special gift"
● crawling on hands and knees while saying "baa"

When you've finished the actions, lead children back to your story area. Gently take the *Learning Mat* down from the wall and set it on the floor or on a table.

Say: **Let's make the sheep and shepherds on our *Learning Mat* look real by decorating them.**

Pass out crayons and markers and let the children color the scene with the shepherds. Then let them take turns gluing some of their fiberfill onto the sheep in the picture. If you have more children than sheep, have two or three children work on one sheep together. Or add extra sheep by gluing some of the fiberfill onto the *Learning Mat* around the sheep that are shown on the mat. As children work remind them that  the shepherds were glad that Jesus is God's special gift.

 **The Point**

When children have finished decorating the shepherds and sheep, give each child a *star sticker* to place in the sky. Say: **Wow! Our *Learning Mat* looks so special. I wonder if our friend Whiskers would like to see it. Maybe we could tell him about the shepherds who saw baby Jesus.**

✔ If your class is large, you could divide the class into two or three groups. Have one group decorate the mat while the others play Follow the Shepherd. Let groups switch activities every few minutes.

✔ If more than one class uses the *Learning Mat* on your lesson day, color only a portion of it and explain that other children will finish the sheep and shepherd picture later. More sheep and stars can be added as necessary.

Practicing The Point

Woolly Whiskers (up to 5 minutes)

Before class, tape fiberfill stuffing all over Whiskers. He should look like a mouse in sheep's clothing! Bring out Whiskers and go through the following puppet script. When you finish the script, put Whiskers away and out of sight.

Woolly Whiskers

PUPPET SCRIPT

Whiskers: Hi, everybody!

Teacher: *(Smiling)* Why, Whiskers, you look different today!

Whiskers: Do you like it? I saw you playing Follow the Shepherd. I love games and I love sheep. So I wanted to dress up like one!

Teacher: Well, you certainly do look woolly! You'd blend right into our *Learning Mat*. Children, let's show Whiskers the *Learning Mat* picture we decorated today.

(Invite two or three children to help you hold up the *Learning Mat*.)

(Continued)

✏ The Point

Whiskers: (*To the children*) Wow! You made this? (*Points to sheep on mat.*) Look, a whole flock of sheep! (*Claps hands.*) Oh, this is so much fun!

Teacher: Whiskers, you said you saw us playing the game. Did you hear our Bible story about the shepherds?

Whiskers: No, I didn't hear a story. But you know I love Bible stories! Tell me, tell me!

Teacher: Let's ask your friends if they can tell you what happened to the shepherds in our Bible story today.
(*Help children tell Whiskers how an angel appeared and told the shepherds that Jesus had been born. Explain how the shepherds hurried to Bethlehem and found baby Jesus, just like the angel said.*)

Whiskers: Boy, that's a good story. The shepherds must have felt important. They got to see baby Jesus first!

Teacher: Yes, Whiskers, ✏ the shepherds were glad that Jesus is God's special gift.

Whiskers: Hmm . . . (*Gets quiet.*)

Teacher: What are you thinking, Whiskers?

Whiskers: Well, the shepherds were lucky. God thought they were important. I wish I was one of them. Sometimes I don't feel very important.

Teacher: Whiskers, the shepherds probably didn't feel very important either. But they were important to God. We're all important to God—even the littlest and the quietest people in our class are important.

Whiskers: Well, that's me! (*Looking around at everyone*) I'm the littlest! You're all bigger than I am.

Teacher: But you're important, Whiskers. Remember the shepherds!

Whiskers: (*Brightens.*) Yes, I'll remember the shepherds. Boy, thanks for telling me! I'm glad that Jesus is God's special gift, too. Hey, everybody, you wanna be sheep together and make sheep praises to God? Baa! Baa-aa!
(*Have children join in with Whiskers.*)

Whiskers: This was fun! I learned a lot today. Bye, everybody! See you next week!

Jesus is God's special gift.

TODAY I LEARNED . . .

We believe Christian education extends beyond the classroom into the home. Photocopy the "Today I Learned..." handout (p. 57) for this week and send it home with your children. Encourage parents to use the handout to plan meaningful family activities to reinforce this week's topic. Follow up the "Today I Learned..." activities next week by asking children what their families did.

Closing

Five Happy Shepherds (up to 5 minutes)

Help children use washable markers to draw two eyes and a smiling mouth on each finger. Say: **Everyone hold up all five fingers. We're going to learn a fun finger play about the shepherds now.**

Lead children in the following finger play. Repeat the rhyme several times so children can learn the words and finger motions.

Five good shepherds watching their sheep. *(Hold up five fingers.)*
One saw the angel, and up he leaped. *(Put other fingers down and hold up only one finger, starting with the thumb.)*
"Come," said the angel, "the Savior is here." *(Beckon with other hand.)*
Away went the shepherd, without any fear. *(Move hand behind back with thumb still up.)*

Repeat the rhyme, holding up four, three, two, then one finger. Finish with this verse:

Five good shepherds standing in a row. *(Hold up all five fingers.)*
They all found Jesus and bowed down low. *(Fold fingers down, making a fist.)*
"We love you, Lord Jesus, we love you, we do." *(Wiggle fingers excitedly.)*
"We'll tell our families and other people, too."

Ask:
● **How did the shepherds feel when they were told about Jesus being born?** (Happy; excited; important.)

Say: ✎**The shepherds were glad that Jesus is God's special gift. Let's fold up our shepherd fingers and thank God for sending Jesus. Thank you, Lord, for giving us the most special gift of all—your Son, Jesus. Amen.**

● **The Point**

For Extra Time

If you have a long class time or want to add additional elements to your lesson, try one of the following activities.

LIVELY LEARNING: Angel Calling

Have everyone be shepherds and lie on the floor pretending to be asleep. Choose one child to be the angel. When the angel says, "Jesus is born," the shepherds are to jump up and follow the angel around the room. When the angel lies down on the floor, everyone else is to lie down, too. Repeat the game and choose a new angel each time. As children play the game, remind them that Jesus is God's special gift.

The Point

MAKE TO TAKE: Thumb-Print Sheep

Give each child a sheet of green construction paper. Show children how to make thumb-print sheep bodies using the *ink pad* in the Learning Lab. Demonstrate how to add a print from a smaller fingertip for the sheep's head. Let children make as many sheep as they want. If they're interested, let them add legs and faces with fine-tipped markers. As children work, review how the shepherds left their sheep to go see baby Jesus. Remind children that the shepherds knew that Jesus is God's special gift.

TREAT TO EAT: Fuzzy Sheep

Combine 1 cup peanut butter, ⅓ cup powdered milk, and honey to taste. Stir to make a dough-like mixture. Add more powdered milk as needed to keep it from being too pasty. If you have more than 15 children in your class, you may need to make additional batches of dough.

Give each child a spoonful of the peanut butter mixture on a small paper plate, along with a spoonful of coconut or powdered sugar, and some raisins. Show children how to roll their peanut butter dough into a ball and then roll it in coconut or powdered sugar to make a fuzzy sheep. Add the raisins for eyes and eat!

Be sure to have wet paper towels on hand for cleaning up sticky fingers.

STORY PICTURE: Angels Tell Shepherds Jesus Is Born

Give each child a copy of the "Today I Learned..." handout (p. 57). Set out crayons or markers and have children color their pictures. Then set out craft sticks and glue and help each child glue a craft stick to the shepherd's staff in the picture. As children work, review how the shepherds hurried to see baby Jesus. Remind children that the shepherds were glad that Jesus is God's special gift.

The Point

Permission to photocopy this handout from Group's Hands-On Bible Curriculum™ for Preschool granted for local church use. Copyright © Group Publishing, Inc., Box 481, Loveland, CO 80539.

TODADY I LEARNED . . .

The Point ● The shepherds were glad that Jesus is God's special gift.

LESSON 3

Today your child learned that the shepherds were glad that Jesus is God's special gift. Children heard how an angel told the shepherds that Jesus was born. They learned a finger play about the shepherds' story and thanked God for sending Jesus.

Verse to Learn

"My heart rejoices in God my Savior" (Luke 1:47).

Ask Me . . .

● How did the shepherds feel when the angel told them that Jesus was born?

● Tell me about a time you felt special and important.

● What can our family do this week to thank God for sending Jesus?

Family Fun

● Practice this finger play with your child. Ask your child to help you with the motions.

Five good shepherds watching their sheep. *(Hold up five fingers.)*

One saw the angel, and up he leaped. *(Put fingers down and hold up thumb.)*

"Come," said the angel, "the Savior is here." *(Beckon with other hand.)*

Away went the shepherd, without any fear. *(Move hand behind back with thumb still up.)*

Angels Tell Shepherds Jesus Is Born (Luke 2:8-15)

Praising the Savior

The Bible Basis

Luke 2:15-20. The shepherds worship Jesus.

The shepherds hurried to find the special baby. Just as the angel had said, they found the baby lying in the manger. As they looked at the tiny child, their hearts were filled with love and praise. Rather than returning quietly to their flocks, the shepherds spread the news that God's promised Savior had arrived. Later, when they went back to their sheep, they continued to praise God for all they had seen and heard.

Three- and 4-year-olds are learning what it means to praise God. They enjoy Bible stories and songs and can pray simple prayers. But they may not connect worship and praising God with Christmas trees and giving gifts. This lesson will show preschoolers how the shepherds praised God on the first Christmas night and encourage them to praise God this Christmas.

Getting The Point

✎ **Jesus is God's special gift, and we worship him.**

It's important to say The Point just as it's written in each activity. Repeating The Point over and over will help the children remember it and apply it to their lives.

Children will
- worship at worship centers,
- hear how the shepherds praised God for sending Jesus,
- help Whiskers remember the true meaning of Christmas, and
- tell another class the good news of Jesus' birth.

✎ **The Point**

This Lesson at a Glance

Before the lesson, collect the necessary items for the activities you plan to use. Refer to the Classroom Supplies and Learning Lab Supplies columns to determine what you'll need. Remember to make photocopies of the "Today I Learned..." handout (p. 72) to send home with your children.

Section	Minutes	What Children Will Do	Classroom Supplies	Learning Lab Supplies
Welcome Time	up to 5	**Welcome!**—Receive name tags and be greeted by the teacher.	"Angel Name Tags" handouts (p. 30)	
Let's Get Started Direct children to one or more of the Let's Get Started activities until everyone arrives.	up to 10	**Option 1: Sing Praise!**—Worship Jesus by singing.	Rhythm instruments, cassette player	Cassette: "Jesus Christ Is Born," "My Heart Rejoices"
	up to 10	**Option 2: Prayerful Praise**—Say prayers of thanks and hear how the shepherds were thankful for Jesus.	Various household items	
	up to 10	**Option 3: Bible-Story Praise**—"Read" Bible Big Books and retell familiar Bible stories.	Adult Bible, children's Bible, Bible Big Books from previous Learning Labs	Bible Big Book: Zacchaeus
Pick-Up Song	up to 5	**Now It's Time**—Sing a song as they pick up toys and gather for Bible-Story Time.	Cassette player	Cassette: "Now It's Time"
Bible-Story Time	up to 8	**Setting the Stage**—Make praying hands and say thank you prayers.	Colored construction paper, scissors, crayons	Gift box, gift bow
	up to 5	**Bible Song and Prayer Time**—Sing a song, bring out the Bible, and pray together.	Bible, cassette player	Angel stamp and ink pad, cassette: "We Are Glad..."
	up to 8	**Hear the Bible Story**—Hear how the shepherds told others about Jesus and name people they can tell.	Bible, praying-hands cutouts from "Setting the Stage," stapler	Learning Mat: Jesus' Birth
	up to 12	**Do the Bible Story**—Share the news about Jesus' birth by singing a song for another class.	Cassette player, rhythm instruments	Cassette: "Jesus Christ Is Born," "My Heart Rejoices"
Practicing The Point	up to 5	**The Best News**—Help Whiskers remember what Christmas is all about.	Whiskers the Mouse	
Closing	up to 5	**Special Gift Prayers**—Remind each other that Jesus is God's special gift.	Praying-hands cutouts from "Setting the Stage"	Gift box, gift bow
For Extra Time	For extra-time ideas and supplies, see page 70.			

Welcome Time

Welcome! (up to 5 minutes)

- Bend down and make eye contact with children as they arrive.
- Greet each child individually with an enthusiastic smile.
- Thank each child for coming to class today.
- As children arrive, ask them about last week's "Today I Learned..." discussion. Use questions such as "What did you tell your family about the shepherds?" or "Did you have fun teaching your family our finger play about the shepherds? Who did the finger play with you?"
- Say: **Today we're going to learn that ✐ Jesus is God's special gift, and we worship him.**
- Hand out the angel name tags children made during Lesson 1 and help them attach the name tags to their clothing. If some of the name tags were damaged or if children weren't in class that week, have them make new name tags using the photocopiable handout on page 30.
- Direct children to the Let's Get Started activities you've set up.

● The Point

Let's Get Started

Set up one or more of the following activities for children to do as they arrive. After you greet each child, invite him or her to choose an activity.

Circulate among the children to offer help as needed and direct children's conversation toward the point of today's lesson. Ask questions such as "How would you feel if you were with the shepherds who saw baby Jesus?" or "What's one way you can tell Jesus you love him?"

✔ Each Let's Get Started option in this lesson introduces children to a different aspect of worship. If possible, set up all three options. If you don't have regular adult helpers in your class, ask a teen or parent to assist with the "Prayerful Praise" activity. Introduce children to the "Bible-Story Praise" activity and then move on to the "Sing Praise!" activity while children "read" the Bible stories on their own.

☐ OPTION 1: Sing Praise! (up to 10 minutes)

Tell children that ✐ Jesus is God's special gift, and we worship him. Explain that one way we can worship Jesus is by singing songs to him.

Sing the songs children have learned during this module's lessons, "Jesus Christ Is Born" and "My Heart Rejoices." Both songs are recorded on the *cassette tape*. Encourage the children to name other familiar praise songs or Christmas carols they'd like to sing. Bring out blocks or rhythm instruments for children to play as they sing.

● The Point

Sing

Jesus Christ is born!
Jesus Christ is born!
Born today in Bethlehem,
Jesus Christ is born!

Lying in a manger,
Lying in a manger,

Born today in Bethlehem,
Jesus Christ is born!

Glory to God!
Glory to God!
Born today in Bethlehem,
Jesus Christ is born!

Sing

My heart re-joices.
My heart re-joices.

My heart re-joices
In God my Savior!

(Repeat twice)

☐ OPTION 2: Prayerful Praise (up to 10 minutes)

Tell children that after the shepherds found baby Jesus, they thanked God. Explain that we can pray and thank God, too. Set out various household items such as a piece of fruit, a toy, a bandage, a Bible, a pair of gloves, and an umbrella. Hold up the items one at a time and talk about what each item can remind us to thank God for. After discussing the items, take time to pray with the children. If children are shy or don't know how to pray, let them hold the items and say, "Thank you, God, for (name of item)." Or have children pray out loud with you or repeat after you. Encourage children to thank God for Jesus, God's special gift.

● **The Point**

☐ OPTION 3: Bible-Story Praise (up to 10 minutes)

Set out an adult Bible, one or two children's Bibles, and the *Bible Big Book: Zacchaeus*. If you've used Hands-On Bible Curriculum for Preschool in previous quarters, you may also want to set out additional *Bible Big Books*.

Tell children that today they'll be learning that ● Jesus is God's special gift, and we worship him. Explain that one way we can worship Jesus is by reading the Bible. Hold up the adult Bible. Explain to children that even though they can't read the words in an adult Bible yet, they can "read" the children's Bibles and *Bible Big Books* by looking at the pictures and telling the stories in their own words. Be sure to remind them that the stories in the *Bible Big Books* come from God's Word, the Bible. Telling the Bible stories now will help them read from the Bible when they get bigger.

✔ You may want to let the children take turns "reading" the *Bible Big Books* to Whiskers.

When everyone has arrived and you're ready to move on to Bible-Story Time, encourage the children to finish what they're doing and get ready to clean up.

Jesus is God's special gift.

Pick-Up Song

Now It's Time (up to 5 minutes)

Lead children in singing "Now It's Time" with the *cassette tape*, to the tune of "The Mulberry Bush." Encourage children to sing along as they help clean up the room.

Sing

Now it's time to clean up our room,
Clean up our room,
Clean up our room.
Now it's time to clean up our room
And put our things away.

Will you help me? Yes, I will.
Yes, I will.
Yes, I will!
Will you help me? Yes, I will.
I'll help you right away.

(Repeat)

Bible-Story Time

Setting the Stage (up to 8 minutes)

Before class, fold sheets of colored construction paper in half. You'll need two folded sheets for each child.

Tell children you'll clap three times to get their attention. Explain that when you clap three times, the children are to stop what they're doing and repeat the clap. Practice this signal a few times. Encourage children to respond quickly so you'll have time for all the fun activities you've planned.

Gather the children around you and ask:

● **What did you do when you came to our class today?** (Sang songs; prayed; told Bible stories.)

Say: **Some of you practiced singing songs to Jesus. Some of you looked at Bible stories in *Bible Big Books*. Some of you prayed thank you prayers. If you prayed thank you prayers, raise your hands and say, "Thank you, God!"**

Pause for children to say, "Thank you, God!" Then say: **Now let's all say that together. Thank you, God!**

You were all learning important things about our Bible story. Today we're going to hear more about what the shepherds did after they found baby Jesus. We'll learn that ◐ Jesus is God's special gift, and we worship him. We've already been worshiping Jesus by singing, praying thank you prayers, and reading Bible stories.

Bring out the *gift box* from the Learning Lab. Hold the box up and ask: **Remember our pretty *gift box*? It reminds us that ◐ Jesus is God's special gift. In our other lessons we had glitter glue, *hay*, and cotton in the box to remind us of different parts of our Bible story. Let's see what's in the box today.**

Ask a child to open the box and hand it to you. Hold it up so children can

◐ **The Point**

◐ **The Point**

● The Point

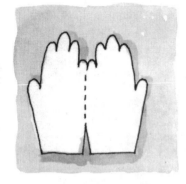

see that it's empty. Say: **That's funny. Our box is empty today. I guess we need to make something to go inside. Today we're learning that ●Jesus is God's special gift, and we worship him.** Ask:

● **What could we make that would help us remember to worship Jesus?** (A book; a church; a Christmas tree.)

Say: **There are lots of ways we can worship Jesus. We can worship him by singing, by coming to church, or by showing his love to people around us. The shepherds worshiped Jesus by thanking God that Jesus had come. Let's make praying hands to remind us to pray and thank God for Jesus. We can put the praying hands in our *gift box*.**

Pass out crayons and the folded construction paper. Have each child slip one sheet inside the other then place one hand on the paper, fingers together and little finger on the fold. Trace around each child's hand. Let children color their hands as you go around and cut the hand tracings out. Cut through both layers of construction paper so each child has two praying-hands cutouts. Put children's names on their cutouts.

When children have finished coloring their hands, clap three times and wait for them to repeat the clap. Say: **Let's put our praying hands in our *gift box* now. We'll each put one praying-hands cutout in the box. I'd like you to keep your other praying hands quietly in your lap so you'll be ready to use them during our Bible story.**

Collect one praying-hands cutout from each child and then lay the cutouts in the *gift box*. As you put the cutouts in the box, have children say with you, "Thank you, God, for Jesus."

Bible Song and Prayer Time (up to 5 minutes)

Say: **Now it's time to choose a Bible person to bring me the Bible marked with today's Bible story. As we sing our Bible song, we'll pass around our special Bible. The person who's holding the Bible when the music stops will be our Bible person today.**

Lead children in singing "We Are Glad to Read the Bible" with the *cassette tape,* to the tune of "Did You Ever See a Lassie?" As you sing, pass around the special Bible.

Sing

We are glad to read the Bible,	We'll hear Bible stories
The Bible, the Bible.	And learn about God's love.
We are glad to read the Bible	We are glad to read the Bible
For it is God's Book.	For it is God's Book.

When the music stops, invite the child who's holding the Bible to bring it to you. Stamp the child's hand with the *angel stamp* and thank the child for bringing you the Bible. Then stamp the other children's hands. Return the *angel stamp and ink pad* to the Learning Lab.

Say: **I'm thankful for** (name of child who brought the Bible) **and I'm thankful for everyone in our class today. Let's thank God together for all our friends in this class.**

Lead children in singing "We Are Glad to Pray Together" with the *cassette tape,* to the tune of "Did You Ever See a Lassie?" If you want to include the names of all the children in your class, sing the song without the cassette and repeat the naming section. If you choose to use the cassette, vary the names you use each week.

Sing

We are glad to pray together,
Together, together.
We are glad to pray together
And give thanks to God.

Lead children in folding their
hands and bowing their heads as
you continue to sing.

Thank you for (name),
And (name), and (name).
Thank you, God, for every person
Who's here in our class.

(Repeat)

Hear the Bible Story (up to 8 minutes)

Bring out the *Learning Mat* and hang it on the wall in the story area. Open your Bible to Luke 2 and show it to the children. Say: **Our Bible story comes from the book of Luke in the Bible. Our *Learning Mat* shows us pictures of our Bible story.**

Point to the *Learning Mat* on the wall. Say: **Look at our beautiful *Learning Mat!* You've all worked so hard to make it special.**

Point to the picture of the angel and Mary. Ask:

● **What is the angel telling Mary?** (That Jesus was coming; that she would be Jesus' mother.)

Point to the picture of the manger scene. Ask:

● **What happened here?**

Give children time to talk about Jesus being born in a stable. Then say: **Mary and Joseph walked all the way to Bethlehem. There was no room for them in the inn. Someone let them stay in a stable, and that's where Jesus was born.**

Point to the picture of the shepherds and sheep. Ask:

● **Who can tell me about this part of our story?**

Let children tell you how the angel came to the shepherds and told them to look for baby Jesus in a manger.

Say: **Yes, the angel came to the shepherds while they were taking care of their sheep. The angel told the shepherds how to find Jesus. Our story today is about something else the shepherds did.**

After the angels went back to heaven, it was dark and quiet again in the fields. The shepherds left their sheep and ran all the way to Bethlehem to find Mary and Joseph and baby Jesus. Let's stand up and pretend we're running with them.

Have children stand up and run in place for a few moments then sit down. Continue: **They ran down the hillside and into Bethlehem. Where did the angel tell them to look for baby Jesus?** (In the stable; in a manger.)

The shepherds looked and looked until they found a baby that was wrapped up in cloth and lying in a manger. Point to the picture of Jesus on the *Learning Mat.* **It was baby Jesus, just as the angels had promised! The shepherds knew right away that ⬤Jesus is God's special gift. After they had seen baby Jesus, they left the stable and went to tell everyone about**

● **The Point**

him. "Jesus is born!" they told people. Turn to someone next to you and tell them, "Jesus is born!"

Let children tell each other "Jesus is born!" and then continue: **People were surprised and happy to hear the shepherds' news about Jesus. As the shepherds went back to their sheep, they thanked God that Jesus had come.** Ask:

● **How did the shepherds feel when they found Jesus?** (Happy; excited; surprised.)

● **When you get a new present that you're excited about, what are some things you do?** (Say thank you; play with it; tell my friends.)

Say: **Sometimes when we get special gifts or surprises we want to go tell our friends about them. We also say thank you to the person who gave us the gift or surprise. That's what the shepherds did. They told others about Jesus and thanked God for him. You know, we can tell people about Jesus, just like the shepherds did. We can tell our friends and families that ◐Jesus is God's special gift, and we worship him at Christmas and all year long.**

You've been holding your praying hands so patiently. I'd like you to think of one person you'd like to tell about Jesus. Maybe you'd like to go home and tell your mom or dad the story we've learned about baby Jesus. Or maybe you want to tell a friend at preschool or in your neighborhood. When you've thought of someone, hold up your praying hands.

As children begin to hold up their praying-hands cutouts, invite them to tell you the person they're thinking of. If children can't think of anyone, suggest that they tell their families. When everyone has named a person, say: **Let's put our praying hands on our *Learning Mat* to help us remember that we can tell people about Jesus, just as the shepherds did.**

Invite children to bring their praying hands to you. Staple the hands around the outside of the *Learning Mat*. Then say: **We can tell people about Jesus, and we can thank God for sending Jesus. Let's fold our hands and do that right now. Dear God, we know that Jesus is your special gift. Thank you for sending him. Help us worship Jesus all year long. In Jesus' name, amen.**

◐ The Point

Do the Bible Story (up to 12 minutes)

◐ The Point

Before class, arrange with another teacher for your children to come and sing a few songs to their class. (An adult class would be as delighted by this as a children's class.)

Say: ◐**Jesus is God's special gift, and we worship him. One way we can worship Jesus is by telling other people about him, just as the shepherds did. In just a few minutes, we're going to go to another class and tell them about Jesus. We're going to sing the songs about Jesus that we've been learning.**

Practice singing "Jesus Christ Is Born" and "My Heart Rejoices" with the *cassette tape*. Each song is recorded on the cassette twice. Pass out blocks or rhythm instruments and let the children use them as they sing.

When the children are ready, lead them to the other classroom and sing the two songs.

Jesus is God's special gift.

Sing

Jesus Christ is born!
Jesus Christ is born!
Born today in Bethlehem,
Jesus Christ is born!

Lying in a manger,
Lying in a manger,

Born today in Bethlehem,
Jesus Christ is born!

Glory to God!
Glory to God!
Born today in Bethlehem,
Jesus Christ is born!

Sing

My heart re-joices.
My heart re-joices.

My heart re-joices
In God my Savior!

(Repeat twice)

When you return to the classroom have the children gather in your story area. Say: **You sang so well. I'm very proud of you.** Ask:

● **How did you feel about singing to the other class?** (A little scared; it was fun.)

Say: **The shepherds in our story made people happy by telling them about Jesus. You were like the shepherds. You made people happy today by singing to them about Jesus.**

Say: ✎**Jesus is God's special gift, and we worship him. We worship Jesus when we sing about him. Let's sing one of our songs again and see if our friend Whiskers will come out. We can tell him about Jesus, too.**

Let children pick their favorite song. Sing a few lines with them, then bring out Whiskers.

✎ **The Point**

Practicing The Point

The Best News (up to 5 minutes)

Bring out Whiskers the Mouse and go through the following puppet script. When you finish the script, put Whiskers away and out of sight.

The Best News

PUPPET SCRIPT

Whiskers: What's that singing I heard? That sounded so pretty. Oh, I'm so excited to see you today!

Teacher: Hello, Whiskers. We're happy to see you, too.

Whiskers: I have the greatest news! I've been waiting all morning to come and tell you! My family opened our Christmas presents, and I got a new blue bike! Just what I've been wanting!

(Continued)

Jesus is God's special gift.

Teacher: Oh, Whiskers, that's special. You must be very happy!

Whiskers: I'm so happy I want to tell everyone I know!

Teacher: Whiskers, you remind me of the shepherds in our Bible story today.

Whiskers: The shepherds? Why?

Teacher: Children, why don't some of you tell Whiskers how the shepherds felt when they found baby Jesus. Tell him what they did after they found him.
(Help the children tell Whiskers how happy the shepherds were to find Jesus and how they hurried to tell everyone about him.)

Whiskers: That *is* exciting! And they were just like me! They had to tell everyone the news!

✏ The Point

Teacher: Yes, Whiskers. The shepherds wanted everyone to know that ⬤ Jesus is God's special gift, and we worship him.

Whiskers: You know, sometimes at Christmastime, I get so excited about all my presents—it's all I think about. Then I forget that Jesus is God's special gift. That's why we have Christmas. *(To a child)* Do you ever forget that we have Christmas to celebrate Jesus' birthday? I do too. *(To another child)* How about you? Do you forget that Jesus is the best present of all?
(Have Whiskers ask several children if they forget about Jesus' birthday at Christmas, then continue.)

Whiskers: Hey, I have an idea!

Teacher: What's that?

Whiskers: We should help each other remember! *(To the children)* Do you want to help me, and I'll help you? Oh, goody! Let's all say together, "Jesus is God's special gift." *(Pause.)* Oh, boy! That was good. Let's say it again, "Jesus is God's special gift."

Teacher: That was a good idea, Whiskers.

Whiskers: Let's keep reminding each other, OK? I've got to go now. I'm going to Cousin Joey's. I'm going to tell him about my new bike and about Jesus being the best gift of all! Goodbye, everybody!

TODAY I LEARNED . . .

We believe Christian education extends beyond the classroom into the home. Photocopy the "Today I Learned..." handout (p. 72) for this week and send it home with your children. Encourage parents to use the handout to plan meaningful family activities to reinforce this week's topic. Follow up the "Today I Learned..." activities next week by asking children what their families did.

Closing

Special Gift Prayers (up to 5 minutes)

Bring out the *gift box* with the praying-hands cutouts children made earlier. Remove one cutout from the box.

Say: 🔵 **Jesus is God's special gift, and we worship him. Let's pray and thank God for sending Jesus right now. I'm going to pass around our** *gift box.* **When it comes to you, take out one praying-hands cutout and give it to me. I'll read the name on the praying hands and say, "Jesus came for** (name on hands cutout)**. Then we'll all say together, "Thank you, God, for Jesus." Let's try that together.**

Say again, "Jesus came for (name on hands cutout)" and then return the hands cutout to its owner. Have children say with you, "Thank you, God, for Jesus." Continue passing the box around until you've returned all the hands cutouts.

Jesus is God's special gift.

For Extra Time

If you have a long class time or want to add additional elements to your lesson, try one of the following activities.

LIVELY LEARNING: Five Happy Shepherds

The Point

Repeat the shepherd finger play. After you do the finger play, remind children that ●Jesus is God's special gift, and we worship him.

Five good shepherds watching their sheep. *(Hold up five fingers.)*
One saw the angel, and up he leaped. *(Put other fingers down and hold up only one finger, starting with the thumb.)*
"Come," said the angel, "the Savior is here." *(Beckon with other hand.)*
Away went the shepherd, without any fear. *(Move hand behind back with thumb still up.)*

Five good shepherds standing in a row. *(Hold up all five fingers.)*
They all found Jesus and bowed down low. *(Fold fingers down, making a fist.)*
"We love you, Lord Jesus, we love you, we do." *(Wiggle fingers excitedly.)*
"We'll tell our families and other people, too."

MAKE TO TAKE: Christmas Lacing Cards

The Point

Before class, punch holes around the edges of small paper plates. Photocopy the "We Worship Jesus" handout (p. 71) and cut out the manger scene. Cut 18- to 20-inch lengths of red or green yarn. You'll need one paper plate, one handout, and one length of yarn for each child. You may want to wrap tape around the ends of the yarn for easier lacing.

Show children how to glue the pictures to their plates then lace the yarn through the holes in the plates. As children work, review how the shepherds worshiped baby Jesus. Remind them that ●Jesus is God's special gift, and we can worship him, too. When children have put the yarn through all the holes, help them tie or tape the ends to the back side of the plate. Loop another piece of yarn through the top hole as a hanger.

TREAT TO EAT: Banana Mangers

Cut peeled bananas in half and then in half again, as shown in the margin. Give each child a banana quarter and several shredded wheat mini-squares. Let children crumble their shredded wheat to make hay. As they're crumbling the cereal, put a thin line of honey on each child's banana. Have children put their shredded wheat hay into their banana mangers and eat. As they enjoy the snack, remind them that the shepherds found baby Jesus lying in a manger.

STORY PICTURE: The Shepherds Worship Jesus

The Point

Give each child a copy of the "Today I Learned..." handout (p. 72). Set out glue and small scraps of fabric and show children how to glue fabric bits onto the shepherds' clothing. Then set out crayons or markers and let children color the picture. As they work, talk about how the shepherds worshiped Jesus. Remind them that ●Jesus is God's special gift, and we worship him.

Jesus is God's special gift.

We Worship Jesus

Photocopy the handout and cut out the picture.

Permission to photocopy this handout from Group's Hands-On Bible Curriculum™ for Preschool granted for local church use.
Copyright © Group Publishing, Inc., Box 481, Loveland, CO 80539.

TODAY I LEARNED . . .

The Point ● Jesus is God's special gift, and we worship him.

Today your child learned that Jesus is God's special gift, and we worship him. Children heard how the shepherds worshiped and thanked God for Jesus. They worshiped by singing, praying, and telling another class about the good news of Jesus' birth.

Verse to Learn

"My heart rejoices in God my Savior" (Luke 1:47).

Ask Me . . .

● What did the shepherds do after they saw baby Jesus?

● What do you do when you receive a special gift?

● How can our family worship Jesus this Christmas?

Family Fun

● Have fun doing this finger play with your child. Then talk about people your family could tell about Jesus' birth this Christmas.

Five good shepherds standing in a row. (*Hold up all five fingers.*)

They all found Jesus and bowed down low. (*Fold fingers down, making a fist.*)

"We love you, Lord Jesus, we love you, we do." (*Wiggle fingers excitedly.*)

"We'll tell our families and other people, too."

The Shepherds Worship Jesus (Luke 2:15-20)

Permission to photocopy this handout from Group's Hands-On Bible Curriculum™ for Preschool granted for local church use. Copyright © Group Publishing, Inc., Box 481, Loveland, CO 80539.

LESSON 4

Gifts of Love

The Bible Basis

Matthew 2:1-12. The wise men worship Jesus.

The wise men had studied, discussed, and prepared for the birth of the foretold king of the Jews with great anticipation. A star in the east led them to Jerusalem where Herod's priests and scribes gave them the last bit of direction they needed—to travel to Bethlehem, the City of David. As they set out, the same star that signaled the birth of the child went on before them, until it stood over the place where the child was. Upon seeing the infant king, they realized that their hopes and dreams had been fulfilled. As they offered their gifts, they bowed down and worshiped him.

Three- and 4-year-olds know what it's like to wait and watch for something special to happen. They wait to bring home and decorate the Christmas tree; then they wait to open the shiny packages that rest beneath it. Like the wise men, they also experience great joy when Christmas day finally arrives. When we celebrate the most special Christmas gift of all, God's Son, we can worship him and give him gifts of love as the wise men did. Use this lesson to encourage children to give Jesus the gift of their love this Christmas.

Getting The Point

✎ **Jesus is God's special gift, and we love him.**

It's important to say The Point just as it's written in each activity. Repeating The Point over and over will help the children remember it and apply it to their lives.

Children will
● follow a star as the wise men did,
● hear how the wise men worshiped Jesus,
● make gifts of love for friends and family, and
● help Whiskers learn that the best gift to give Jesus is our love.

✎ **The Point**

This Lesson at a Glance

Before the lesson, collect the necessary items for the activities you plan to use. Refer to the Classroom Supplies and Learning Lab Supplies columns to determine what you'll need. Remember to make photocopies of the "Today I Learned..." handout (p. 87) to send home with your children.

Section	Minutes	What Children Will Do	Classroom Supplies	Learning Lab Supplies
Welcome Time	up to 5	**Welcome!**—Receive name tags and be greeted by the teacher.	"Angel Name Tags" handouts (p. 30)	
Let's Get Started Direct children to one or more of the Let's Get Started activities until everyone arrives.	up to 10	**Option 1: Loving Hearts**—Make fingerprint hearts to show that they love Jesus.	"Loving Hearts" handouts (p. 84), scissors	Ink pad
	up to 10	**Option 2: Camel Rides**—Carry each other on "camels" and hear how the wise men traveled to Bethlehem.	Blankets	
	up to 10	**Option 3: Stencil Stars**—Make star pictures and hear how the wise men followed a star.	Poster board, masking tape, damp sponges, colored chalk	
Pick-Up Song	up to 5	**Now It's Time**—Sing a song as they pick up toys and gather for Bible-Story Time.	Cassette player	Cassette: "Now It's Time"
Bible-Story Time	up to 5	**Setting the Stage**—Follow a path of stars to the Learning Mat.	Red and yellow construction paper, cassette player, scissors, "Shining Star" handouts (p. 85)	Gift box, gift bow, Learning Mat, cassette: "We Three Kings"
	up to 5	**Bible Song and Prayer Time**—Sing a song, bring out the Bible, and pray together.	Bible, cassette player	Angel stamp and ink pad, cassette: "We Are Glad..."
	up to 10	**Hear the Bible Story**—See and hear how the wise men worshiped Jesus and then decorate the wise men on the Learning Mat.	Bible, "Gifts of Love" handout (p. 86), green and red construction paper, scissors, crayons, markers, fabric scraps, foil, glitter glue, cassette player	Learning Mat, cassette: "We Three Kings"
	up to 8	**Do the Bible Story**—Make edible gifts of love to share.	Sweet clay ingredients (p. 80)	
Practicing The Point	up to 5	**A Perfect Gift**—Help Whiskers decide what to give Jesus.	Whiskers the Mouse, three small toys	
Closing	up to 5	**Hearts of Love**—Pass a heart around a circle and tell Jesus they love him.	Paper heart used earlier, glue	Gift box, Learning Mat, cassette: "My Heart Rejoices"
For Extra Time		For extra-time ideas and supplies, see page 83.		

Jesus is God's special gift.

Welcome Time

Welcome! (up to 5 minutes)

- Bend down and make eye contact with children as they arrive.
- Greet each child individually with an enthusiastic smile.
- Thank each child for coming to class today.
- As children arrive, ask them about last week's "Today I Learned..." discussion. Use questions such as "What did you tell your family about the shepherds?" or "How did your family worship Jesus this week?"
- Say: **Today we're going to learn that** **Jesus is God's special gift, and we love him.**
- Hand out the angel name tags children made during Lesson 1 and help them attach the name tags to their clothing. If some of the name tags were damaged or if children weren't in class that week, have them make new name tags using the photocopiable handout on page 30.
- Direct children to the Let's Get Started activities you've set up.

● The Point

Let's Get Started

Set up one or more of the following activities for children to do as they arrive. After you greet each child, invite him or her to choose an activity.

Circulate among the children to offer help as needed and direct children's conversation toward the point of today's lesson. Ask questions such as "What gift could you give Jesus?" or "How could you show Jesus that you love him?"

OPTION 1: Loving Hearts (up to 10 minutes)

Before class, photocopy the "Loving Hearts" handout (p. 84) and cut out the heart. You'll need one handout for each child.

Read children the words on the handout and then talk with them about ways they can show they love Jesus. Then help them use the *ink pad* from the Learning Lab to make fingerprint hearts, as shown in the margin illustration. Let them decorate their heart shapes with as many heart fingerprints as they want. As children work, remind them that ● Jesus is God's special gift, and we love him. Suggest that they put their hearts under their Christmas trees as birthday gifts for Jesus.

> ✔ Children will need help making the fingerprint hearts. Guide their fingers and help them make one or two hearts, then let them try making their own. If fingerprint hearts are too difficult for some children, encourage them to make a border of individual fingerprints near the edge of the heart.
>
> ✔ If you wish, provide red or green construction paper hearts for children to glue their finished heart handouts onto.

OPTION 2: Camel Rides (up to 10 minutes)

Lay an old blanket or a sturdy sheet on the floor. Tell children that today they'll learn about some men who traveled a long way to see baby Jesus. Explain that the men may have traveled on camels. Have one child sit in the middle of the blanket while other children pull the blanket "camel" around the room. Let children take turns riding the "camel." As they play, point out that the wise men didn't mind traveling for a long time because they knew that Jesus is God's special gift.

> ✔ For even more camel-ride fun, invite one or two parents to come and give children camel rides on their backs.

OPTION 3: Stencil Stars (up to 10 minutes)

Give each child an 8-inch poster-board square and at least six pieces of masking tape. Show children how to apply the masking tape to the poster board to create a star shape. Then invite children to help you rub colored chalk on several damp sponges. Help them press the sponges all over their taped poster-board squares. The chalk will stick to the paper.

As you carefully peel off the masking tape to reveal the stencil stars, explain to the children that today they'll hear a story about some men who followed a star to find baby Jesus. Remind them that Jesus is God's special gift, and we love him.

> ✔ Don't leave the masking tape on the poster board for too long, or it won't come off easily.
>
> ✔ If you leave little edges of tape sticking up, it will be easier to peel off.

When everyone has arrived and you're ready to move on to Bible-Story Time, encourage the children to finish what they're doing and get ready to clean up.

Pick-Up Song

Now It's Time (up to 5 minutes)

Lead children in singing "Now It's Time" with the *cassette tape*, to the tune of "The Mulberry Bush." Encourage children to sing along as they help clean up the room.

Jesus is God's special gift.

Sing

Now it's time to clean up our room,	Will you help me? Yes, I will.
Clean up our room,	Yes, I will.
Clean up our room.	Yes, I will!
Now it's time to clean up our room	Will you help me? Yes, I will.
And put our things away.	I'll help you right away.

(Repeat)

Bible-Story Time

Setting the Stage (up to 5 minutes)

Before class, place a red construction paper heart and a yellow construction paper star inside the *gift box* from the Learning Lab. Photocopy the "Shining Star" handout (p. 85) on yellow paper and cut out the stars. You'll need eight or ten stars. As children are cleaning up their Let's Get Started activities, use the stars to make a trail around the room. Start the trail in your story area. Hide the *Learning Mat* at the end of the trail.

Tell the children you'll clap your hands three times to get their attention. Explain that when you clap your hands, the children are to stop what they're doing and repeat the clap. Practice this signal a few times. Encourage children to respond quickly so you'll have time for all the fun activities you've planned. Ask:

● **What did you make or do when you came to our class today?** (Made a heart present for Jesus; rode on a blanket; made a star appear.)

Say: **Some of you made fingerprint hearts to show your love for Jesus. Some of you took rides on blanket camels. Some of you made special star pictures. You were all learning important things about our Bible story. Today we're going to learn about some men who traveled a long way to see baby Jesus. They knew that ● Jesus is God's special gift.**

● **The Point**

Bring out the *gift box* with the heart and star inside. Hold up the box and say: **Speaking of gifts, let's see what's in our *gift box*. Our *gift box* should have something in it to help us with our Bible story today.**

Ask a child to open the box and hand you the heart and star. Hold up the heart and say: **A pretty heart! What could this heart have to do with our Bible story about Jesus being born?** (Mary and Joseph loved Jesus; God wants us to love Jesus.)

Then say: ● **Jesus is God's special gift, and we love him. We'll use this heart later to help us tell Jesus we love him. Then we can put it on our *Learning Mat*.**

● **The Point**

Hold up the star and say: **A star. Some of you have already learned about a star today. Raise your hand if you made a star picture.** Pause. **What could a star have to do with our Bible story?** (The men followed the star to find Jesus; it was nighttime.)

Say: **God put a special star in the sky to help the wise men find baby Jesus. I've put some special stars in our classroom to help us find the picture of baby Jesus on our *Learning Mat*. Can you be wise and help** me follow the stars?

Return the star and heart to the *gift box* and set it aside. Have children line up as you begin playing "We Three Kings" on the *cassette tape.* Say: **Is everyone ready? While our music is playing, let's follow the stars and see where they lead us.**

Have children follow you from star to star. In between stars, say things such as "Where do we go from here? Oh, you're right! Good eyes! You're so wise!"

When you reach the last star, have children help you find the *Learning Mat.* Then have children return to your story area. Turn off the cassette and hang the *Learning Mat* on the wall.

Say: **That was fun! You were very wise. You followed the stars to just the right place! Let's get our Bible and find out how the special star helped the wise men find Jesus.**

Bible Song and Prayer Time (up to 5 minutes)

Say: **Now it's time to choose a Bible person to bring me the Bible marked with today's Bible story. As we sing our Bible song, we'll pass around our special Bible. The person who's holding the Bible when the music stops will be our Bible person today.**

Lead children in singing "We Are Glad to Read the Bible" with the *cassette tape,* to the tune of "Did You Ever See a Lassie?" As you sing, pass around the special Bible.

Sing

We are glad to read the Bible,	We'll hear Bible stories
The Bible, the Bible.	And learn about God's love.
We are glad to read the Bible	We are glad to read the Bible
For it is God's Book.	For it is God's Book.

When the music stops, invite the child who's holding the Bible to bring it to you. Stamp the child's hand with the *angel stamp* and thank the child for bringing you the Bible. Then stamp the other children's hands. Return the *angel stamp and ink pad* to the Learning Lab.

Say: **I'm thankful for** (name of child who brought the Bible) **and I'm thankful for everyone in our class today. Let's thank God together for all our friends in this class.**

Lead children in singing "We Are Glad to Pray Together" with the *cassette tape,* to the tune of "Did You Ever See a Lassie?" If you want to include the names of all the children in your class, sing the song without the cassette and repeat the naming section. If you choose to use the cassette, vary the names you use each week.

Jesus is God's special gift.

Sing

We are glad to pray together,
Together, together.
We are glad to pray together
And give thanks to God.

Lead children in folding their
hands and bowing their heads as
you continue to sing.

Thank you for (name),
And (name), **and** (name).
Thank you, God, for every person
Who's here in our class.

(Repeat)

Hear the Bible Story (up to 10 minutes)

Before class, copy the "Gifts of Love" pattern (p. 86) onto green paper. Lay a sheet of red paper behind the green paper and fold them in half together with the red on the inside.

Open your Bible to Matthew 2 and show it to the children. Say: **Our Bible story comes from the book of Matthew in the Bible. Our *Learning Mat* shows us pictures of our Bible story.**

Point to the *Learning Mat* and say: **Look how beautiful our *Learning Mat* looks! Today we'll get to finish it. Listen now as I tell you our Bible story.**

When Jesus was born, only a few people knew he was a special baby. Those people knew that Jesus was God's Son because an angel had told them. Ask:

● **Do you remember who the angel talked to?** (Mary; Joseph; shepherds.)

● **Can you find those people on our *Learning Mat?***

Say: **An angel talked to Mary, to Joseph, and to the shepherds. God also used a special star in the sky to tell some other men about Jesus' birth. The men watched and watched for the star. When they saw the beautiful, big star in the sky, they knew a special baby would be born. So they packed up their camels and started on their way to find baby Jesus. They kept following the star across the sky until it stopped right over the place where baby Jesus was. Can you find baby Jesus on our *Learning Mat?***

As children point to the picture of Jesus in the manger, take the folded green and red paper with the gift pattern copied on it and cut from A to B. Ask:

● **Does anyone know what the wise men brought to Jesus?** (Presents; gold.)

Open up the papers then fold the gift figure back on Lines 1 and 2 so only the gift shows. Hold it up and say: **They brought gifts! The wise men gave baby Jesus special gifts of gold and sweet-smelling perfumes called frankincense** (FRANK-in-sens) **and myrrh** (MUR). **Why do you think they brought gifts to baby Jesus?** (Because they loved him; because it was his birthday.)

Open up the gift figure all the way and then fold it again on the center line with the green side still showing. Cut away Sections 1, 2, and 3 while you say: **The wise men showed their love for Jesus by bringing him gifts.** ✏**Jesus is God's special gift, and we love him, too.** Ask:

● **What gift could you give Jesus this Christmas?** (My toys; love; cookies.)

Open up the papers and fold the red heart sections to the front. The heart halves will meet, showing a red heart against the green gift. Hold it up and say: **There is one thing Jesus wants more than anything else. Jesus**

✏ The Point

wants your love more than anything! Who would like to give Jesus their love? Let's tell Jesus together, "Jesus, we give you our love." Ready? "Jesus, we give you our love."

Pass around the heart and gift shape if the children want to see it. Then set it aside and say: **Now it's time to decorate the last section of our *Learning Mat*. I have crayons and markers for you and some pieces of fabric and things to decorate the wise men with. I'll play our wise-men song while we work.**

Set out markers, crayons, glue, and fabric scraps. If possible, include fabrics such as velvet, satin, or silk. Also set out tape and aluminum foil or Mylar paper for children to decorate the wise men's gifts. Play "We Three Kings" from the *cassette tape* while children work. When they're finished, outline the large star on the mat with glitter glue.

● **The Point**

Say: **Our *Learning Mat* looks great. You've worked hard on it. It shows a lot of love.** ✏ **Jesus is God's special gift, and we love him.** Ask:
● **How did the wise men feel when they finally found Jesus?** (Happy; excited; surprised.)
● **Why did they bring gifts to Jesus?** (They loved him; they wanted to; he was special.)

● **The Point**

Say: **The wise men had waited and waited for Jesus. They knew that** ✏ **Jesus is God's special gift. We've been learning that, too, and we can give Jesus gifts of love this Christmas, just as the wise men did. Let's make some special gifts of love now.**

Do the Bible Story (up to 8 minutes)

Before class, make "sweet clay" by mixing ⅓ cup margarine, ⅓ cup corn syrup, ½ teaspoon of salt, and 1 teaspoon of vanilla or peppermint extract. Add a 1-pound box of powdered sugar and knead until smooth. Divide the clay into several bowls. This recipe makes enough sweet clay for a group of 15 children.

Show children the bowls of clay, then have them help you add food coloring to each bowl. Let children smell the clay, then say: **The wise men brought gifts of love to Jesus. Some of their gifts were sweet-smelling perfumes. We can make gifts to show our love for Jesus, too.** ✏ **Jesus is God's special gift, and we love him. We're going to use this sweet-smelling, sweet-tasting clay to make some treats that will remind us that** ✏ **Jesus is God's special gift. We'll make one gift to keep and one to give away to a friend or family member.**

● **The Point**

● **The Point**

Give each child a paper towel, a plastic knife, and a spoonful of sweet clay. Help children sculpt their clay into hearts, stars, or other shapes that will remind them of today's Bible story. Have children set their finished sculptures on graham crackers. Encourage them to keep one and share one to help a friend or family member remember Jesus' birth.

● **The Point**

Say: ✏ **Jesus is God's special gift, and we love him. As you share your sweet gifts, remember that Jesus is the greatest gift of all.**

Set children's graham crackers aside until the end of class.

Practicing The Point

A Perfect Gift (up to 5 minutes)

Bring out Whiskers the Mouse and three small toys and go through the following puppet script. When you finish the script, put Whiskers away and out of sight.

A Perfect Gift

PUPPET SCRIPT

Whiskers: (*Comes out with small toys in hands. Holds them up, one at a time, looking at them.*) Hmm-mm. Maybe this one. No, maybe this one. Or oh-h, I'm just not sure.

Teacher: Hi, Whiskers. What are you doing?

Whiskers: Well, I heard your Bible story about the wise men. They brought gifts to Jesus. I wanted to give him a gift, too. Which one do you think he'd like best? (*Holds up the toys.*)

Teacher: Whiskers, I think your friends can help you with that. They learned during our Bible-story time that there's one gift that Jesus wants more than anything else.

Whiskers: Oh goody! Tell me, tell me! I want to give Jesus the perfect gift!

Teacher: Children, can you tell Whiskers what gift Jesus wants most?
   (*Lead children to tell Whiskers that the best gift we can give Jesus is our love.*)

Teacher: You see, Whiskers, the wise men gave Jesus gifts because they knew he was special. The shepherds loved and worshiped Jesus, too. So did Mary and Joseph. 🖊 Jesus is God's special gift, and we love him. Our love is the perfect gift for Jesus.

Whiskers: I didn't know that! I do love Jesus.

Teacher: That's great, Whiskers. Just give Jesus your love every day. You'll make him very happy.

Whiskers: You just made me very happy—now I know what to give Jesus! Thanks! Bye!

🖊 **The Point**

Jesus is God's special gift.

TODAY I LEARNED . . .

We believe Christian education extends beyond the classroom into the home. Photocopy the "Today I Learned . . ." handout (p. 87) for this week and send it home with your children. Encourage parents to use the handout to plan meaningful family activities to reinforce this week's topic. Follow up the "Today I Learned . . ." activities next week by asking children what their families did.

Closing

Hearts of Love (up to 5 minutes)

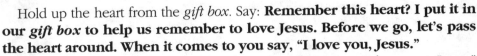

Hold up the heart from the *gift box*. Say: **Remember this heart? I put it in our *gift box* to help us remember to love Jesus. Before we go, let's pass the heart around. When it comes to you say, "I love you, Jesus."**

Pass the heart around and encourage each child to say, "I love you, Jesus." If some children don't want to say it alone, have everyone say it together. When everyone has had a turn, lead children in saying together: ● **Jesus is God's special gift, and we love him.**

Put some glue on the back of the heart. Choose a child to glue the heart above the manger on the *Learning Mat*. Say: **Our *Learning Mat* is all finished now. Isn't it beautiful? You did such fine work.**

Say: **Let's tell Jesus we love him in one more way. Let's worship Jesus by singing "My Heart Rejoices."**

Lead children in singing "My Heart Rejoices" with the *cassette tape*, to the tune of "Ten Little Indians." The song is recorded on the cassette twice.

Sing

My heart re-joices.
My heart re-joices.

My heart re-joices
In God my Savior!

(Repeat twice)

Jesus is God's special gift.

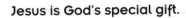

For Extra Time

If you have a long class time or want to add additional elements to your lesson, try one of the following activities.

LIVELY LEARNING: *Learning Mat* Review

Have children gather in the story area and hang the *Learning Mat* on the wall. Let children use the *Learning Mat* to retell the Bible story to Whiskers. They can take turns using Whiskers and telling parts of the story.

As you finish each section, lead children in the corresponding song or rhyme from the list below.

- Lesson 1: "My Heart Rejoices" (p. 15)
- Lesson 2: "Away in a Manger" (p. 36)
- Lesson 3: "Jesus Christ Is Born" (p. 50)
- Lesson 4: Shepherd finger play (p. 55)
- Lesson 5: "We Three Kings" (p. 78)

As children tell the story, lead them in repeating The Point: ✏️Jesus is God's special gift.

● The Point

MAKE TO TAKE: Swirling Stars

Before class, cut newsprint circles to fit into the bottom of a salad spinner. You'll need one newsprint circle for each child in your class.

Let children watch as you place a paper circle in the spinner and then drip a few drops of yellow tempera paint onto the paper. Snap the lid on the spinner and spin the handle. Open the spinner and carefully remove the swirling star print. Remind children that the wise men followed a special star to find Jesus.

Have children form groups of three. Call one group at a time and let children take turns putting in the paper, dripping the paint, and spinning the handle. Let the child who spins the handle remove and keep the swirling star print. While children are waiting, let them make their own star trails around the room with the stars you set out during "Setting the Stage."

TREAT TO EAT: Cheese Stars

Set out star-shaped cookie cutters and cheese slices. Let children use the cookie cutters to cut cheese stars. If you don't have star-shaped cookie cutters on hand, let children use plastic knives to cut the cheese into triangles. Then show them how to put the triangles together to make stars. As children create and enjoy their cheese stars, point out that the wise men followed a special star to find baby Jesus.

STORY PICTURE: Wise Men Bring Gifts to Jesus

Give each child a copy of the "Today I Learned..." handout (p. 87). Set out crayons or markers and invite children to tell you about the wise men as they color their pictures. Then bring out scented extracts or perfumes. Let children choose their favorite smells and help them dab a drop of scent on each of the wise men's gifts. As they work, remind them that ●Jesus is God's special gift, and we love him.

● The Point

Loving Hearts

Photocopy the handout and cut out the heart. Make enough copies for each child to have one.

Jesus, I love you!

Permission to photocopy this handout from Group's Hands-On Bible Curriculum™ for Preschool granted for local church use.
Copyright © Group Publishing, Inc., Box 481, Loveland, CO 80539.

Jesus is God's special gift.

Shining Star

Photocopy and cut out the star. You'll need eight to 10 stars.

Permission to photocopy this handout from Group's Hands-On Bible Curriculum™ for Preschool granted for local church use.
Copyright © Group Publishing, Inc., Box 481, Loveland, CO 80539.

Jesus is God's special gift.

Gifts of Love

Photocopy the handout onto green paper.

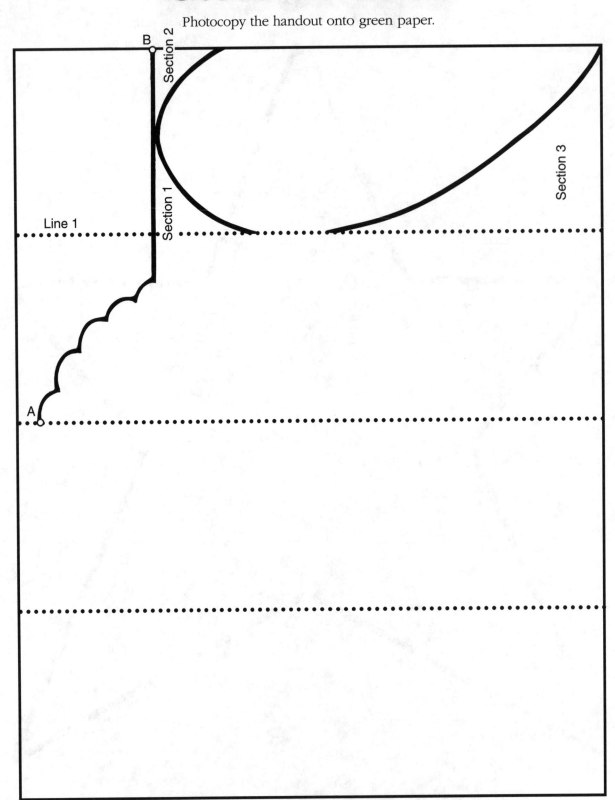

(Pattern adapted from *Clip & Tell Bible Stories,* copyright © 1995 Lois Keffer. Reprinted by permission of Group Publishing, Inc., Box 481, Loveland, CO 80539.)
Permission to photocopy this handout from Group's Hands-On Bible Curriculum™ for Preschool granted for local church use.
Copyright © Group Publishing, Inc., Box 481, Loveland, CO 80539.

Jesus is God's special gift.

TODAY I LEARNED . . .

The Point ● Jesus is God's special gift, and we love him.

Today your child learned that Jesus is God's special gift, and we love him. Children heard how the wise men brought gifts to Jesus. They learned that the best gift to give Jesus is their love.

Permission to photocopy this handout from Group's Hands-On Bible Curriculum™ for Preschool granted for local church use. Copyright © Group Publishing, Inc., Box 481, Loveland, CO 80539.

Verse to Learn

"My heart rejoices in God my Savior" (Luke 1:47).

Ask Me . . .

● What did the wise men do to show their love for Jesus?

● What can you give to show Jesus you love him?

● What can our family do to show Jesus we love him?

Family Fun

● Sing this Scripture song with your child, to the tune of "Ten Little Indians."

My heart re-joices,
My heart re-joices,
My heart re-joices,
In God my Savior.

Wise Men Worship Jesus (Matthew 2:1-12)

Jesus' Miracles

Jesus always made time to meet people's needs. His teaching about God's love warmed their hearts. His gentle, healing touch calmed their fears, soothed their wounds, and banished their diseases. People came to Jesus sick, lonely, even outcast—and went away whole. They came hungry and went away full. They came in despair and left rejoicing. Everywhere Jesus went, he changed people's lives with his miraculous love.

Young children often feel small and powerless in an adult world. They need help with even the simplest of tasks. They'll be comforted to know that Jesus is a friend who can help with any task, no matter how difficult. Use these lessons to teach children that Jesus can do anything, even in our lives today!

Four Lessons on Jesus' Miracles

	Page	The Point	Bible Basis
Lesson 6 **Help and Healing**	97	Jesus can do anything.	John 5:1-9
Lesson 7 **What's for Lunch?**	109	Jesus can do anything.	John 6:1-14
Lesson 8 **The Eyes Have It**	121	Jesus can do anything.	Mark 10:46-52
Lesson 9 **Cast Out Your Net**	133	Jesus can do anything.	John 21:1-13

Time Stretchers

Jesus Is Faithful

Lead children in singing "Jesus Is Faithful" to the tune of "Jesus Loves Me." Explain that when we say Jesus is faithful, we mean that he promises to always take care of us. As you sing, have the children do the simple motions to reinforce the words of the song.

Sing

I was blind and could not see
(cover eyes with hands)
'Til Jesus came and healed me.
(Uncover eyes.)
As a crippled man, I could not stand (squat down)
'Til Jesus took me by the hand.
(Jump up with hands on knees.)

With two fish and five loaves of bread (hold up two fingers, then five),
A great big hungry crowd he fed. (Rub tummy.)
Jesus cares for me and you.
(Point to a friend.)
I know he'll feed my family, too. (Pretend to eat.)

Jesus is faithful,
Yes, he is faithful. (Nod head.)
Jesus is faithful
To care for you and me. (Cross arms in front of self.)

Jesus is faithful,
Yes, he is faithful. (Nod head.)
Jesus is faithful
To care for you and me. (Cross arms in front of self.)

Get-Well Card Center

 **The Point**

As children learn about Jesus' healing miracles, encourage them to comfort people they know who are sick. They can pick people they know individually, or you can check with your pastor to find out about church members who are ill.

Set out colored construction paper, markers or crayons, stickers, the *happy-face stamp and ink pad,* and other art supplies children can use to make get-well cards. As children work, talk with them about times they've been sick and what that was like. Encourage them to pray for the people they know who are sick. Remind them that ✎Jesus can do anything, including healing sick people.

Remembering God's Word

Each four- or five-week module focuses on a key Bible verse. The key verse for this module is "I can do all things through Christ, because he gives me strength" (Philippians 4:13).

This module's key verse will teach children that Jesus' power can help them every day. Enjoy using these ideas any time during the lessons on Jesus' miracles.

Strong Prayers

● **The Point**

Say: **We're learning that ⬤ Jesus can do anything. But did you know that *we* can do anything if we ask Jesus to help us? Listen to what the Bible says about that.**

Read the key verse aloud and then have children repeat it with you. Say: **Nothing is too hard if Jesus is helping us. Let's say a prayer together and ask Jesus to help us this week.**

Have children pray the following prayer with you. After you've prayed it together, invite children to fill in their own situations for the first line. For example, a child might say, "When I go over to my friend Jordan's house" or "When I help take care of my baby brother."

> **When I'm at home, or school, or play,**
> **Lord Jesus, make me strong.**
> **Help me do what's right each day**
> **And trust you all day long.**

Close the activity by repeating the key verse once more.

Jesus Makes Me Strong

● **The Point**

Say: **Did you know that ⬤ Jesus can do anything? He can make sick people well and blind people see. He fed a big crowd of people with one little boy's lunch. And Jesus can help us be strong and do what's right. Listen to what the Bible says about that.**

Read the key verse and then have children repeat it with you. Say: **Let's sing a fun song together to help us learn that Bible verse. We'll hold up our strong arms and march around the room while we sing it.**

Lead children in singing "I Can Do All Things" with the *cassette tape,* to the tune of "Old MacDonald." The song is recorded on the cassette twice.

Encourage children to hold up strong arms as they're marching. Have them use strong voices to shout out the last two lines.

Sing

> **I can do all things through Christ**
> **Because he makes me strong.**
> **Jesus helps me do what's right—**
> **He's with me all day long.**
> **He healed the sick,**
> **Fed the crowd.**
> **Everybody shout out loud:**
> **I can do all things through Christ**
> **Because he makes me strong.**

(Repeat)

Story Enhancements

Make Bible stories come alive in your classroom by bringing in Bible costumes, setting out sensory items, or creating bulletin boards. The following ideas will help you get started.

If children can use their senses to discover what life was like for the people Jesus helped, they'll learn even more. Each week bring in one or more of the following items to enhance the Bible story experience.

Lesson 6
● Bring in a first-aid kit. Talk about the contents of the kit and what each item is used for. Explain that today we use first-aid kits to treat people who are hurt or sick. Tell children that they'll be hearing how Jesus healed a man who had been sick almost his whole lifetime.

● Bring in a woven mat or rug. Let children take turns lying on the mat. Explain that in Jesus' time, people who couldn't walk often lay on mats. Encourage children to help each other up as you tell them how Jesus helped the sick man.

Lesson 7
● Bring in a lunch box or bag and some items you might pack for lunch. Show children the items. Ask them if they think you have enough to share with two or three people. Then ask them if you have enough to share with everyone in the whole church. Explain that Jesus fed more than 5,000 people with one little boy's lunch.

● Bring in a picture of a crowd or a stadium full of people. Show children the picture and explain that a crowd of people gathered around Jesus whenever he taught. Tell children how Jesus fed all the people in the crowd with just five loaves and two fish.

Lesson 8
● Make an eye chart to bring to class. On a large sheet of poster board, make three rows of letters. Make the top row very large, the middle row normal size, and the bottom row smaller than normal. Let the children use the eye chart to test each other's vision. Talk about what it would be like if they couldn't see. Explain that Jesus healed a man who couldn't see anything.

● Bring in a set of watercolor paints and paintbrushes. Set out paper and let children experiment with the colors. Encourage them to try mixing different colors to create new ones. Talk about all the different colors we can see. Explain that Jesus gave sight to a blind man who couldn't see any colors.

Lesson 9
● Bring in fishing equipment such as fishing flies, a fishing vest, and a child's fishing pole. Talk about how you'd prepare to go fishing today—by getting bait, choosing a spot, waking up early—and then going to fish. Point out how disappointing it would be not to catch any fish after all that preparation. Explain that the disciples fished all night, but they didn't catch anything until Jesus told them where to throw their net.

● Bring in a net full of toys or stuffed animals. (If you don't have a net, use a pillowcase.) Let children try to lift the net. Talk about how the disciples' net was heavy when it was full of fish. Explain that their net was so full of fish they couldn't pull it back into the boat.

Jesus Can Do Anything Bulletin Board

Use colored yarn to divide your bulletin board into four equal parts. At the top, post the title: "Jesus Can Do Anything." In the top left square, post the sentence: "Jesus healed the sick." In the top right square, post the sentence: "Jesus fed the crowd." In the bottom left square, post the sentence: "Jesus helped the blind man see." In the bottom right square, post the sentence: "Jesus helped his friends catch fish." Each week add the following items to your bulletin board.

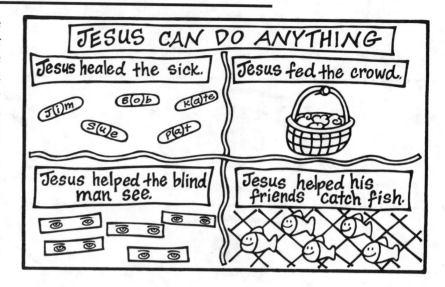

Lesson 6

Use a permanent marker to print each child's name on a brightly colored adhesive bandage. Let children stick their bandages on the bulletin board under the words "Jesus healed the sick." Tell children how Jesus healed a man who had been sick for 38 years.

Lesson 7

Attach a small basket to the bulletin board under the words "Jesus fed the crowd." Let children create pretend barley loaves by crumpling newsprint into balls. Explain that Jesus fed more than 5,000 people with five barley loaves and two small fish. Have children place their "barley loaves" in the basket on the bulletin board.

Lesson 8

Photocopy and cut out the "Seeing Eyes" pattern on page 94. You'll need one pair of seeing eyes for each child. Set out crayons and invite each child to color a set of eyes the same color as his or her own eyes. As they work, talk about all the things they can see in your classroom. Explain that they'll be learning about how Jesus helped a man who couldn't see. Have children attach their finished seeing eyes to the bulletin board by the words "Jesus helped the blind man see."

Lesson 9

Cover the square with the words "Jesus helped his friends catch fish" with netting. If you don't have netting, crisscross the area with string or yarn to make a net pattern. Photocopy the "Fish in a Net" handout on page 95. You'll need to cut out a fish for each child in your class. Let children color the fish and attach them to the net. As they work, tell them how Jesus helped his friends fill their net with fish.

Seeing Eyes

Photocopy and cut out the eyes. You need a pair of eyes for each child.

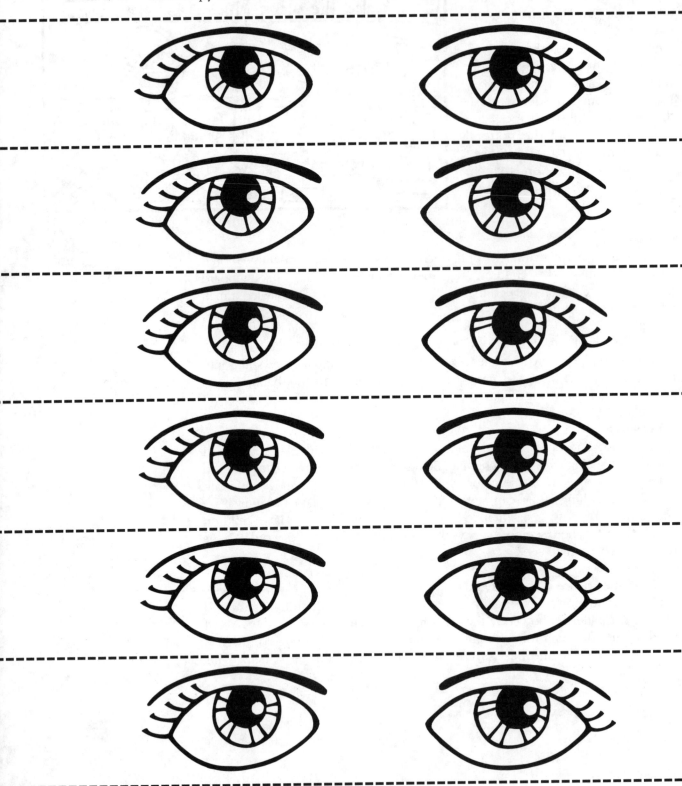

Permission to photocopy this handout from Group's Hands-On Bible Curriculum™ for Preschool granted for local church use.
Copyright © Group Publishing, Inc., Box 481, Loveland, CO 80539.

Fish in a Net

Photocopy and cut out the fish. You need at least one fish for each child.

Permission to photocopy this handout from Group's Hands-On Bible Curriculum™ for Preschool granted for local church use.
Copyright © Group Publishing, Inc., Box 481, Loveland, CO 80539.

Help and Healing

The Point

🖊 Jesus can do anything.

The Bible Basis

John 5:1-9. Jesus heals a man who has been sick for 38 years.

The pool of Bethesda was a breeding ground for sickness and disease. Day after day, sick people crowded around, each hoping to be the first into the pool's swirling, reputedly healing waters. No healthy person would want to approach this germ-infested area—but Jesus did. In the midst of those who were blind, crippled, and paralyzed, Jesus noticed a man who'd spent most of his life suffering. In a moment of compassion, Jesus healed the man, and 38 years of sickness and suffering came to an end. Immediately, the man picked up his mat and walked away.

Three- and 4-year-olds are firmly grounded in the tangible and immediate—waiting 38 years for anything is beyond their comprehension. But they understand what it's like to be sick in bed when they'd rather be out playing. Use this lesson to teach preschoolers that Jesus can help them when they're sick, just as he helped the man by the pool.

Getting The Point

🖊 **Jesus can do anything.**

It's important to say The Point exactly as it's written each time it appears. Repeating The Point over and over will help the children remember it and apply it to their lives.

Children will
- talk about what it might be like to be sick for a long time,
- hear how Jesus healed a man who had been sick for 38 years,
- comfort Whiskers when he's sick, and
- sing a song to celebrate Jesus' miracles.

⬤ **The Point**

This Lesson at a Glance

Before the lesson, collect the necessary items for the activities you plan to use. Refer to the Classroom Supplies and Learning Lab Supplies columns to determine what you'll need. Remember to make photocopies of the "Today I Learned..." handout (p. 108) to send home with your children.

Section	Minutes	What Children Will Do	Classroom Supplies	Learning Lab Supplies
Welcome Time	up to 5	**Welcome!**—Receive name tags and be greeted by the teacher.	"Angel Name Tags" handouts (p. 30)	
Let's Get Started Direct children to one or more of the Let's Get Started activities until everyone arrives.	up to 12	**Option 1: Stir the Waters**—Stir water in a tub and hear how Jesus healed a sick man by a pool.	Towels, shallow tub, water, spoons, spatulas	
	up to 12	**Option 2: Patient Patients**—"Bandage" each other and hear how Jesus healed a sick man.	Rolls of bathroom tissue	
	up to 12	**Option 3: Make-a-Mat**—Make mats and hear how Jesus helped a sick man pick up his mat and walk.	11x17 construction paper, crayons or markers	Happy-face stamp and ink pad
Pick-Up Song	up to 5	**Now It's Time**—Sing a song as they pick up toys and gather for Bible-Story Time.	Cassette player	Cassette: "Now It's Time"
Bible-Story Time	up to 8	**Setting the Stage**—Play a game to discover what makes them feel better when they're sick or hurt.	Mats from Option 3	
	up to 5	**Bible Song and Prayer Time**—Sing a song, bring out the Bible, and pray together.	Bible, cassette player	Happy-face stamp and ink pad, cassette: "We Are Glad ..."
	up to 8	**Hear the Bible Story**—Hear the story from John 5:1-9 about how Jesus healed a man who had been sick for 38 years.	Bible, scissors, masking tape, mats from Option 3	Learning Mat: Jesus Can Do Anything
	up to 5	**Do the Bible Story**—Sing a song and help each other up from their mats.	Cassette player, mats from Option 3	Cassette: "Yes, He Can"
Practicing The Point	up to 5	**Sick Forever!**—Hear how Whiskers has been sick for days and tell him about Jesus' healing power.	Whiskers the Mouse, washcloth	
Closing	up to 5	**Pick-Me-Up Prayers**—Help each other up with a reminder that Jesus can do anything.		
For Extra Time		For extra-time ideas and supplies, see page 106.		

Jesus can do anything.

Welcome Time

Welcome! (up to 5 minutes)

- Bend down and make eye contact with children as they arrive.
- Greet each child individually with an enthusiastic smile.
- Thank each child for coming to class today.
- As children arrive, ask them about last week's "Today I Learned..." discussion. Use questions such as "What did you tell your family about the wise men?" or "How did your family show your love for Jesus this week?"
- Say: **Today we're going to learn that** ⬤ **Jesus can do anything.**
- Hand out the angel name tags children made during Lesson 1 and help them attach the name tags to their clothing. If some of the name tags were damaged or if children weren't in class that week, have them make new name tags using the photocopiable handout on page 30.
- Direct children to the Let's Get Started activities you've set up.

✏ **The Point**

Let's Get Started

Set up one or more of the following activities for children to do as they arrive. After you greet each child, invite him or her to choose an activity.

Circulate among the children to offer help as needed and direct children's conversation toward the point of today's lesson. Ask questions such as "Have you ever been sick? What was that like?" or "What kinds of things can make us feel better when we're sick?"

Option 1: Stir the Waters (up to 12 minutes)

Set out several towels and a shallow plastic tub filled with water. Give children spoons and spatulas and let them stir and play gently in the water. Explain that today they'll hear how Jesus healed a sick man who sat by a special pool of water. The man believed that the moving water could make him well.

Option 2: Patient Patients (up to 12 minutes)

Set out several rolls of bathroom tissue and let children "bandage" each other. Encourage them to take turns being "doctors" and "patients." As they play, talk about how doctors and parents care for them when they're sick. Explain that today they'll learn how Jesus made a sick man well.

Option 3: Make-a-Mat (up to 12 minutes)

Set out 11×17 sheets of colored construction paper, crayons or markers, and the *happy-face stamp and ink pad.* Explain that today's Bible story is about a sick man who lay on a mat by a pool. Let each child decorate a sheet of construction paper to use as a mat during the Bible story. If children finish early they can make a mat for someone else. You'll need a mat for each child in your class.

Jesus can do anything.

✔ If you have mostly 4-year-olds in your class, have children create woven mats. Cut slits in the construction paper and set out 1x17 strips for children to weave through the slits. Three-year-olds may also be able to do this with adult help.

When everyone has arrived and you're ready to move on to Bible-Story Time, encourage the children to finish what they're doing and get ready to clean up.

Pick-Up Song

Now It's Time (up to 5 minutes)

Lead children in singing "Now It's Time" with the *cassette tape,* to the tune of "The Mulberry Bush." Encourage children to sing along as they help clean up the room.

Sing

Now it's time to clean up our room,
Clean up our room,
Clean up our room.
Now it's time to clean up our room
And put our things away.

Will you help me? Yes, I will.
Yes, I will.
Yes, I will!
Will you help me? Yes, I will.
I'll help you right away.

(Repeat)

Bible-Story Time

Setting the Stage (up to 8 minutes)

Tell the children you'll clap your hands three times to get their attention. Explain that when you clap your hands, the children are to stop what they're doing and repeat the clap. Practice this signal a few times. Encourage children to respond quickly so you'll have time for all the fun activities you've planned. Ask:

● **What did you make or do when you came to our class today?** (Played in water; put a bandage on someone; made a mat to sit on.)

Say: **If you stirred the water, stand and twirl your arms around in a circle and then sit down.** Pause. **If you bandaged someone or got a bandage, stand up and show us your bandage and then sit down.** Pause. **If you made a mat, stand up and hold it high over your head and then sit down on it.**

Say: **You were all learning important things about our Bible story. Today we're going to learn that ●Jesus can do anything. We'll hear**

✏ **The Point**

how Jesus met a sick man by a pool and made him well. Ask:

● **What's it like to be sick?** (Boring; yucky; you have to stay in bed.)
● **What are some things that help you get well when you're sick?** (Medicine; going to the doctor; resting.)

Pass out mats to any children who didn't make them earlier. Say: **I'm going to read a list of things you might do to help you get well when you're sick. If I read something that will really help you get well, stand up. If I read something that won't help you get well, stay seated on your mat.**

● **drinking juice**
● **going swimming**
● **going to the doctor**
● **climbing a tree**
● **medicine from your doctor**

● **riding your tricycle**
● **resting quietly**
● **eating lots of candy**
● **asking Jesus to help**

● The Point

Say: **Jesus can help us when we're sick or hurt because ✎ Jesus can do anything. Let's all sit down on our mats now and get ready to hear our Bible story. We're going to hear how Jesus helped a man who had been sick for a long, long time.**

Bible Song and Prayer Time (up to 5 minutes)

Say: **Now it's time to choose a Bible person to bring me the Bible marked with today's Bible story. As we sing our Bible song, we'll pass around our special Bible. The person who's holding the Bible when the music stops will be our Bible person today.**

Lead children in singing "We Are Glad to Read the Bible" with the *cassette tape,* to the tune of "Did You Ever See a Lassie?" As you sing, pass around the special Bible.

Sing

We are glad to read the Bible,
The Bible, the Bible.
We are glad to read the Bible
For it is God's Book.

We'll hear Bible stories
And learn about God's love.
We are glad to read the Bible
For it is God's Book.

When the music stops, invite the child who's holding the Bible to bring it to you. Stamp the child's hand with the *happy-face stamp* and thank him or her for bringing you the Bible. Then stamp the other children's hands. Return the *happy-face stamp and ink pad* to the Learning Lab.

Say: **I'm thankful for** (name of child who brought the Bible) **and I'm thankful for everyone in our class today. Let's thank God together for all our friends in this class.**

Lead children in singing "We Are Glad to Pray Together" with the *cassette tape,* to the tune of "Did You Ever See a Lassie?" If you want to include the names of all the children in your class, sing the song without the cassette and repeat the naming section. If you choose to use the cassette, vary the names you use each week.

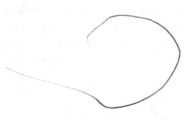

Jesus can do anything.

Sing

We are glad to pray together,
Together, together.
We are glad to pray together
And give thanks to God.

Lead children in folding their
hands and bowing their heads as
you continue to sing.

Thank you for (name),
And (name), and (name).
Thank you, God, for every person
Who's here in our class.

(Repeat)

Hear the Bible Story (up to 8 minutes)

Before class, cut apart the two halves of the *Learning Mat: Jesus Can Do Anything.* Open the perforated windows on the top half of the mat, then lay the window section over the bottom section of the mat. Fasten the two sections together at the top with masking tape. As you open each window, children will be able to see the results of Jesus' miracles.

Have children gather around the *Learning Mat.* Open your Bible to John 5:1-9 and show it to the children. Say: **Our story comes from the book of John in the Bible, God's special book. Our *Learning Mat* shows us pictures of our Bible story.**

Raise your hand if you've ever been sick. Let children respond. **Now, keep your hand up if you've ever gone to the doctor when you were sick.** Ask:

● **Why do we go to the doctor?** (To find out what's wrong; to make us better.)

Say: **That's right. When we're sick we usually go to the doctor so the doctor can tell us what we can do to feel better. But in Bible times, doctors didn't always know how to help sick people.**

Point to the pool on the *Learning Mat.* Say: **Do you see this pool? Well, sick people thought that the water from this pool could make them well. They thought that when the water was moving, whoever got into the pool first would be healed. So every day many sick people sat by the pool and waited for the water to move. When the water moved, everyone hurried to be the first one into the water. Let's pat our hands on our legs and pretend like we're hurrying to get into the pool.** Pause. **Do you think going swimming in a pool can make you better when you're sick?** Let children respond.

Say: **There was one man by the pool who had been sick for 38 years. Let's find him here on our *Learning Mat.*** Have children point out the sick man lying near Jesus.

Say: **Thirty-eight years is a long, long time. For you, that would be like getting sick today and staying sick until you were all grown up. Show me what you would look like if you'd been sick all that time.** Let children show their sick faces to you and to each other.

Say: **One day Jesus came to the pool. He noticed all the sick people—especially the man who had been sick for 38 years. The sick man was lying on a mat. Let's lie down on our mats and pretend we're the sick man.**

Let children lie down, then continue. **Jesus asked the sick man, "Do you want to be well?" The man said, "Yes, but I can't get into the pool fast**

Jesus can do anything.

enough. No one will help me. So when the water moves, someone else always gets there first."

So Jesus said to the man, **"Stand up. Pick up your mat and walk."** Right away, the man was well. **When I count to three, let's all jump up from our mats like the sick man did and say, "Thank you, Jesus!" One, two, three.** Jump up. **Thank you, Jesus!**

Say: **Show me how you'd look if Jesus had just made you well.** Pause. **Let's see how the sick man looked after Jesus healed him.**

Open the window to reveal the man standing beside Jesus with his mat. Then say: **Look how happy and thankful the man looks now.** 🖊 **Jesus can do anything—even heal a man who has been sick for 38 years! Let's play a game now to help us remember this story.**

🖊 **The Point**

Do the Bible Story (up to 5 minutes)

Say: **We're going to learn a fun song to help us remember that** 🖊 **Jesus can do anything. Everyone find a spot in the room and lie down on your mat. As we sing the song, I'll come around and help you up from your mat, just as Jesus helped the sick man. After you get up, you can help me help others up from their mats.**

🖊 **The Point**

Lead children in singing "Yes, He Can" with the *cassette tape,* to the tune of "London Bridge." The song is recorded on the cassette three times. Each time you sing, "Jesus can do anything!" help another child stand and join your line. Encourage children to clap when the song says, "Clap your hands!"

If you have more than 12 students in your class, you may want to have children join your line two at a time.

Sing 🎵🎵🎵🎵🎵🎵🎵🎵🎵🎵🎵🎵🎵🎵🎵🎵🎵🎵🎵🎵🎵🎵

Jesus can do anything!
Yes, he can! Clap your hands!
Jesus can do anything!
Yes, he can!

Jesus can do miracles!
Yes, he can! Clap your hands!
Jesus can do miracles!
Yes, he can!

After all the children have joined your line, say: **That was fun!** 🖊 **Jesus can do anything. When we're sick or hurt, we can pray for Jesus to help us. Speaking of being sick, I heard that our friend Whiskers hasn't been feeling too well lately. Maybe we could see if he's feeling any better today. Let's go quietly back to our story area in case he's resting.**

🖊 **The Point**

Practicing The Point

Sick Forever! (up to 5 minutes)

Before class, fold a washcloth in half and drape it over Whiskers head.

After you get back to the story area and everyone is seated quietly, say: **Let's see if Whiskers is feeling well enough to come out and visit with us. So we don't scare him, let's whisper and say, "Whiskers, Whiskers."**

Jesus can do anything.

Lead children in whispering for Whiskers, then bring him out and go through the following script. When you finish the script, put Whiskers away and out of sight.

Sick Forever!

PUPPET SCRIPT

Whiskers: (With washcloth draped over his head and moaning) Ohhh...hello, boys and girls...ohhh...

Teacher: Hi, Whiskers. It sounds like you're still not feeling well.

Whiskers: Ohhh...I've been so sick. I feel just awful!

Teacher: Goodness, Whiskers, tell us what's wrong.

Whiskers: I have a terrible earache! My mom took me to the doctor yesterday, and she gave me some medicine that will help me feel better in a day or two. But I don't know if I can wait that long.

Teacher: Oh, I'm so sorry you've been sick. It's no fun to have an earache, is it, boys and girls? (Let children respond.) Sometimes when we're sick it seems like we'll never get well. Today we heard a story about a man who had been sick for a very long time. Children, let's tell Whiskers how long the man in our story had been sick.
   (Help children tell Whiskers about the man who had been sick for 38 years.)

Whiskers: Thirty-eight years! That's a long time. My mom isn't even 38 years old! I hope I'm not sick for that long. What happened to the man? Is he still sick? Did he ever get better? What kind of medicine did he have to take?

Teacher: Actually, he got better and he didn't even need any medicine. Boys and girls, let's tell Whiskers how the man got well.
   (Help children tell Whiskers how Jesus healed the man.)

Whiskers: That's great! You mean Jesus healed him just like that? He didn't have to wait for any medicine to work or anything?

Teacher: That's right. He got well right away. Jesus can do that. ⬛ Jesus can do anything. Let's all say that together.
   (Lead the children and Whiskers in repeating The Point.)

Whiskers: Wow! ⬛ Jesus can do anything! I think I'll go home right now and ask my mom to read me that story from my Bible storybook. I can lie down and rest while she reads it. I'll see you next week. Goodbye!

⬛ **The Point**

⬛ **The Point**

Jesus can do anything.

TODAY I LEARNED ...

We believe Christian education extends beyond the classroom into the home. Photocopy the "Today I Learned..." handout (p. 108) for this week and send it home with your children. Encourage parents to use the handout to plan meaningful family activities to reinforce this week's topic. Follow up the "Today I Learned..." activities next week by asking children what their families did.

Closing

Pick-Me-Up Prayers (up to 5 minutes)

Have children sit in a circle. Say: **Let's help each other up before we say a prayer together. I'll stand up and say,** ✏️ **"Jesus can do anything!" Then I'll help** (name of child on your right) **stand up. Then** (name of child) **will help the next person in our circle stand up. When it's your turn to help someone stand up, say,** ✏️ **"Jesus can do anything!" and then help that person up.**

Stand and help the child next to you stand up, as you say, ✏️ "Jesus can do anything." Continue around the circle until everyone is standing, then close with a prayer similar to this one: **Dear Jesus, thank you for all the great things you do for us. We know you take care of us and help us when we're sick. You can do anything. We love you. Amen.**

✏️ **The Point**

✏️ **The Point**

✏️ **The Point**

For Extra Time

If you have a long class time or want to add additional elements to your lesson, try one of the following activities.

LIVELY LEARNING: Bandage on the Boo-Boo

Before class, draw an outline of a person on a sheet of newsprint and hang it at children's eye level. Ask children what part of the person may be sick or hurt. If they need help, suggest things such as scraped knees or elbows, tummy aches, or earaches.

Mark the "hurt" spots with red crayon and then have children line up. Hand each child a bandage. Have children take turns closing their eyes and trying to put bandages on the marked "hurt" spots. As children play the game, point out that we use medicine and bandages to help us feel better. Remind children that  Jesus can do anything, and he can make us feel better when we're sick, too.

MAKE TO TAKE: Get-Well Door Hangers

Before class, photocopy the "Get Well!" handout (p. 107) and cut out the door-hanger pattern. You'll need one door hanger for each child.

Set out crayons, markers, other art supplies, and the *happy-face stamp and ink pad*. If you've used Hands-On Bible Curriculum for Preschool before, you may want to set out other stamps and ink pads as well. Let children decorate their door hangers with the supplies you've set out. As they work, talk about what it's like to be sick and have someone cheer you up. Review how Jesus made the sick man well. Encourage children to use their door hangers to cheer up a sick friend or family member.

TREAT TO EAT: Thirty-Eight Snacks

Set out 38 pieces of a small snack such as grapes, raisins, or crackers. Have children help you count the pieces, then give each child two or three pieces to eat. If you have a large class, you may need to provide additional pieces. As children count the pieces, talk about how Jesus healed the man who had been sick for 38 years. Remind children that Jesus can do anything.

STORY PICTURE: "I'm Healed!"

Give each child a copy of the "Today I Learned..." handout (p. 108). Set out crayons and markers and have children color the picture. Then set out fabric scraps for children to glue to the sick man's mat. As they work, talk about how excited the man must have been to finally be well. Remind children that Jesus can do anything.

The Point

The Point

The Point

Jesus can do anything.

Get Well!

Photocopy the handout and cut out the door-hanger pattern. You'll need one door hanger for each child in your class.

Permission to photocopy this handout from Group's Hands-On Bible Curriculum™ for Preschool granted for local church use.
Copyright © Group Publishing, Inc., Box 481, Loveland, CO 80539.

Jesus can do anything.

TODAY I LEARNED . . .

The Point ● Jesus can do anything.

Today your child learned that Jesus can do anything. Children heard how Jesus healed a man who had been sick for 38 years. They talked about times they've been sick and thanked Jesus for taking care of them.

Verse to Learn

"I can do all things through Christ, because he gives me strength" (Philippians 4:13).

Ask Me . . .

● Why did sick people come to the pool?

● Tell me about a time when you were sick. What made you feel better?

● How can we help when someone in our family is sick?

Family Fun

● Gather 38 beans and use them to help your child count to 38. Explain that the man Jesus healed had been sick for 38 years. Point out that the man must have been very happy to finally be well. Use the beans to make a smiling face, then thank Jesus for taking care of your family members when they get sick.

Jesus Heals a Sick Man (John 5:1-9)

Permission to photocopy this handout from Group's Hands-On Bible Curriculum™ for Preschool granted for local church use. Copyright © Group Publishing, Inc., Box 481, Loveland, CO 80539.

What's for Lunch?

The Point

📝 Jesus can do anything.

The Bible Basis

John 6:1-14. Jesus feeds more than 5,000 people.

As word of Jesus' healing miracles spread, crowds of people began to follow Jesus wherever he went. Some may have been seeking healing; others simply wanted to catch a glimpse of a famous miracle worker. Looking over the hungry crowd, Jesus knew it would take a miracle to provide enough food for everyone. A boy came forward to offer his lunch—two fish and five small barley loaves. Jesus took this meager lunch, thanked God for it, then passed pieces of the bread and fish throughout the crowd. In an astonishing display of divine power, Jesus fed over 5,000 people, and his disciples gathered 12 baskets of leftovers.

Three- and 4-year-olds love to hear how a child's generosity helped Jesus perform a great miracle. They may not fully grasp the size of the crowd that Jesus fed, but they know that, without God's power, one person's lunch doesn't go far. This lesson will teach children how Jesus' power helped a crowd of people and encourage them to trust Jesus for help in their own lives.

Getting The Point

📝 **Jesus can do anything.**

It's important to say The Point exactly as it's written each time it appears. Repeating The Point over and over will help the children remember it and apply it to their lives.

Children will
- hear how Jesus fed 5,000 people with one small lunch,
- experience sharing food with other children,
- help Whiskers understand Jesus' great miracle, and
- sing a song to celebrate Jesus' miracle.

⬤ **The Point**

This Lesson at a Glance

Before the lesson, collect the necessary items for the activities you plan to use. Refer to the Classroom Supplies and Learning Lab Supplies columns to determine what you'll need. Remember to make photocopies of the "Today I Learned..." handout (p. 120) to send home with your children.

Section	Minutes	What Children Will Do	Classroom Supplies	Learning Lab Supplies
Welcome Time	up to 5	**Welcome!**—Receive name tags and be greeted by the teacher.	"Angel Name Tags" handouts (p. 30)	
Let's Get Started Direct children to one or more of the Let's Get Started activities until everyone arrives.	up to 12	**Option 1: Many From Few**—Make two fish into many and hear how Jesus used fish to feed a crowd of people.	Colored yarn, scissors, tape	
	up to 12	**Option 2: Lunch Time**—Fix pretend lunches and hear how Jesus used one boy's lunch to feed a crowd.	Toy dishes, pretend food	
	up to 12	**Option 3: Something for Everyone**—Break bread into many pieces and hear how Jesus broke loaves of bread to feed a crowd.	Paper plates, bread slices	
Pick-Up Song	up to 5	**Now It's Time**—Sing a song as they pick up toys and gather for Bible-Story Time.	Cassette player	Cassette: "Now It's Time"
Bible-Story Time	up to 5	**Setting the Stage**—Share pieces of bread.	Bread pieces from Option 3	
	up to 5	**Bible Song and Prayer Time**—Sing a song, bring out the Bible, and pray together.	Bible, cassette player	Happy-face stamp and ink pad, cassette: "We Are Glad..."
	up to 8	**Hear the Bible Story**—Hear how Jesus fed 5,000 people.	Bible, "Miracle Fish" pattern (p. 119), scissors	Learning Mat: Jesus Can Do Anything
	up to 5	**Do the Bible Story**—Sing an action song to review the Bible story.	Cassette player	Cassette: "The Miracle Lunch"
Practicing The Point	up to 8	**Many Meals for Mice**—Teach Whiskers how Jesus fed many people with a small amount of food.	Whiskers the Mouse	
Closing	up to 5	**Miracle Lunch**—Sing a song and thank God for miracles.	Cassette player	Cassette: "The Miracle Lunch"
For Extra Time		For extra-time ideas and supplies, see page 118.		

Jesus can do anything.

Welcome Time

Welcome! (up to 5 minutes)

- Bend down and make eye contact with children as they arrive.
- Greet each child individually with an enthusiastic smile.
- Thank each child for coming to class today.
- As children arrive, ask them about last week's "Today I Learned..." discussion. Use questions such as "What did you tell your family about the sick man?" or "How did the sick man get well?"
- Say: **Today we're going to learn that ⬤ Jesus can do anything.**
- Hand out the angel name tags children made during Lesson 1 and help them attach the name tags to their clothing. If some of the name tags were damaged or if children weren't in class that week, have them make new name tags using the photocopiable handout on page 30.
- Direct children to the Let's Get Started activities you've set up.

⬤ **The Point**

Let's Get Started

Set up one or more of the following activities for children to do as they arrive. After you greet each child, invite him or her to choose an activity.

Circulate between the activities to offer help as needed and direct children's conversation toward the point of today's lesson. Ask questions such as "How much food do you think we'd need to feed everyone in our church?" or "How many people could eat if we had just one lunch to share?"

▢ OPTION 1: Many From Few (up to 12 minutes)

Before class, cut two 36-inch lengths of colored yarn. Lay each length of yarn on a table in a fish shape, as shown in the margin illustration.

Tell children that they're going to make these two fish into many more fish. Cut each length of yarn into six to nine pieces and show children how to make each piece into a fish shape. You may need to tape the small fish to the table to help them retain their shape. As children fill the table with fish, explain that today's Bible story is about a time Jesus fed a crowd of people with two fish and five loaves of bread.

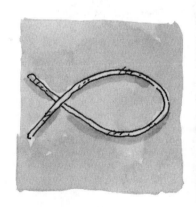

✔ If children enjoy making the fish shapes, you may want to cut additional 4- to 6-inch lengths of yarn and let them make more fish.

▢ OPTION 2: Lunch Time (up to 12 minutes)

Set out toy dishes and pretend food and let children take turns fixing each other picnic lunches. As they play, talk with them about places they like to go for picnics and foods they like to take with them. Explain that today's Bible story is about a time Jesus used one boy's picnic lunch to feed a whole crowd of people.

☐ OPTION 3: Something for Everyone (up to 12 minutes)

Set out two paper plates and five slices of bread. Break the bread into pieces so that each child has one piece. Have children wash their hands, then give them the bread pieces. Have children break the bread into smaller pieces and put the smaller pieces on the paper plates. When the bread is broken into pieces, ask the children if they think that these two plates of food could feed all the people in the church. Explain that today's Bible story is about how Jesus fed a meal to a crowd of people with five small loaves of bread and two little fish.

When everyone has arrived and you're ready to move on to Bible-Story Time, encourage the children to finish what they're doing and get ready to clean up.

Pick-Up Song

Now It's Time (up to 5 minutes)

Lead children in singing "Now It's Time" with the *cassette tape,* to the tune of "The Mulberry Bush." Encourage children to sing along as they help clean up the room.

Sing 🎵

Now it's time to clean up our room,
Clean up our room,
Clean up our room.
Now it's time to clean up our room
And put our things away.

Will you help me? Yes, I will.
Yes, I will.
Yes, I will!
Will you help me? Yes, I will.
I'll help you right away.

(Repeat)

Bible-Story Time

Setting the Stage (up to 5 minutes)

Tell children you'll clap your hands three times to get their attention. Explain that when you clap your hands, the children are to stop what they're doing and repeat the clap. Practice this signal a few times. Encourage children to respond quickly so you'll have time for all the fun activities you've planned. Ask:

● **What did you make or do when you came to our class today?** (Made string fish; made a pretend lunch; put pieces of bread on plates.)

Say: **Some of you made a few fish into lots of fish, some of you made** a few pieces of bread into lots of bread pieces, and some of you got ready to go on pretend picnics. You were all learning important things about our Bible story.

If you packed a pretend picnic, stand up, rub your tummy, and say "yum-yum," then sit down. Pause. If you made a few fish into lots of fish, stand up and swim over to the table, then swim back and sit down. Pause. If you helped make bread pieces, help carry the plates to me. Thank you. Now you may sit down.

Wait for the children to bring you the bread pieces and sit down. Then pass the plates around and let each child sample a few pieces. As they eat, ask:

● **Do you think these bread pieces would be enough for lunch?**

● **Do you think these bread pieces could feed 100 people? one thousand people?**

Let children respond, then say: **Today we're going to hear how Jesus made lunch for more than 5,000 people with just two fish and five loaves of bread. We couldn't make our bread pieces feed 5,000 people, but Jesus could.**  **Jesus can do anything. Let's bring out our Bible now and hear how he fed all those people.**

● The Point

Bible Song and Prayer Time (up to 5 minutes)

Say: **Now it's time to choose a Bible person to bring me the Bible marked with today's Bible story. As we sing our Bible song, we'll pass around our special Bible. The person who's holding the Bible when the music stops will be our Bible person today.**

Lead children in singing "We Are Glad to Read the Bible" with the *cassette tape,* to the tune of "Did You Ever See a Lassie?" As you sing, pass around the special Bible.

Sing

We are glad to read the Bible,	We'll hear Bible stories
The Bible, the Bible.	And learn about God's love.
We are glad to read the Bible	We are glad to read the Bible
For it is God's Book.	For it is God's Book.

When the music stops, invite the child who's holding the Bible to bring it to you. Stamp the child's hand with the *happy-face stamp* and thank him or her for bringing you the Bible. Then stamp the other children's hands. Return the *happy-face stamp and ink pad* to the Learning Lab.

Say: **I'm thankful for** (name of child who brought the Bible) **and I'm thankful for everyone in our class today. Let's thank God together for all our friends in this class.**

Lead children in singing "We Are Glad to Pray Together" with the *cassette tape,* to the tune of "Did You Ever See a Lassie?" If you want to include the names of all the children in your class, sing the song without the cassette and repeat the naming section. If you choose to use the cassette, vary the names you use each week.

Sing

We are glad to pray together,
Together, together.
We are glad to pray together
And give thanks to God.

Lead children in folding their
hands and bowing their heads as
you continue to sing.

Thank you for (name),
And (name), and (name).
Thank you, God, for every person
Who's here in our class.

(Repeat)

Hear the Bible Story (up to 8 minutes)

Before class, photocopy the "Miracle Fish" pattern (p. 119) and cut out only the outline of the fish. Have the fish and a pair of scissors ready nearby.

Gather the children around the *Learning Mat: Jesus Can Do Anything.* Open the Bible to John 6:1-14 and show it to the children. Say: **Our story comes from the book of John in the Bible, God's special book. Our *Learning Mat* shows us pictures of our Bible story.**

Say: **Raise your hand if you've ever been on a picnic.** Ask:

● **What do you like to eat when you go on a picnic?** (Sandwiches; peanut butter and jelly; cookies.)

● **Where do you like to go to eat your picnic lunch?** (Outside; to the park; in my back yard.)

Say: **Well today we're going to pretend that we're all on a picnic. Let's pretend that we've been listening to Jesus all morning, and he's teaching us lots of things about God's love. It's great to sit outside on the soft, green grass and listen to Jesus! But we've been sitting here for a long time, and we're starting to get hungry. When I count to three, let's all rub our tummies and say, "Ohh, I'm hungry!" One, two, three.**

Lead children in rubbing their tummies and saying, "Ohh, I'm hungry!" Then point to the picture of Jesus and the crowd on the *Learning Mat.*

Say: **Look at these people on our *Learning Mat.* Do you think they look hungry? They were hungry all right. But all the people were so excited about listening to Jesus that they had forgotten to bring any food!** Ask:

● **What do you think they did?** (They went to the store; they went home to get some.)

Say: **They didn't have fast-food restaurants in Jesus' time. They didn't even have refrigerators or grocery stores. There was no place for all those people to buy food. So Jesus sent his helpers into the crowd to find out if anyone had any food to share. Turn to the person next to you and ask, "Do you have any food?"** Pause.

Hold up the fish pattern. Say: **Jesus' helpers found one little boy who had two little fish and five loaves of bread. The little boy was glad to share his lunch. But do you think two little fish and five loaves of bread would feed all those people?**

Begin cutting the fish along the lines at both edges as you continue: **Jesus said a prayer to thank God for the two fish and five loaves of bread. Then he asked his helpers to start passing out the fish and bread. They thought for sure they were going to run out, but they just kept passing**

Jesus can do anything.

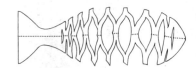

and passing. **Let's pretend we're passing out bread and fish. Take a piece of bread and pass it down. Now take a piece of fish and eat it.**

Let children pretend to pass the bread and fish as you finish cutting the fish pattern. Stretch out the fish. Say: **Guess what? All the people in the crowd had enough to eat. Jesus made two fish and five loaves of bread stretch to feed more than 5,000 people! Jesus' helpers even picked up 12 baskets of leftovers. Jesus can do anything—even turn a little lunch into enough food to feed a hungry crowd.**

Let's open the window on our *Learning Mat* to see how the people looked after Jesus fed them. Show me what you look like after you've eaten a good lunch.

As children show full or satisfied expressions, open the window to reveal the smiling, happy crowd. Say: **When Jesus fed all those people, he did a miracle. That means he did something great that no one else can do. We couldn't make two fish and five loaves of bread feed that many people, but Jesus did. Jesus can do anything. Let's sing a song to help us remember how Jesus fed the crowd.**

Do the Bible Story (up to 5 minutes)

Say: **Jesus can do anything. He fed more than 5,000 people with just two fish and five loaves of bread. Let's sing a song about that miracle lunch. First you can do the motions with me and then sing along.**

Lead children in singing "The Miracle Lunch" with the *cassette tape*, to the tune of "Old MacDonald." The song is recorded on the cassette twice. As you sing, do the motions as indicated.

Sing

A little boy said, "Here, take my lunch *(hold out hands, palms up)*;
I'm really glad to share." *(Nod head.)*
And with that lunch, Jesus fed the whole bunch *(sweep right arm in front of you)*—
Every person there. *(Sweep left arm in front of you.)*
With five little loaves *(hold up five fingers on right hand)*
And two little fish *(hold up two fingers on left hand)*—
Here a loaf *(hold out right hand, palm up)*,
There a fish *(hold out left hand, palm up)*—
Mmm, that's a yummy dish! *(Rub tummy.)*
Jesus made a miracle lunch *(point up to heaven)*
When a little boy said, "I'll share." *(Hold out both hands, palms up.)*

(Repeat)

Turn off the cassette and say: **Our friend Whiskers loves to go on picnics. I bet he'd like to hear our story about the miracle lunch. When I count to three, let's call for Whiskers. One, two, three: Whiskers! Whiskers!**

Lead children in calling for Whiskers.

Practicing The Point

Many Meals for Mice (up to 8 minutes)

Bring out Whiskers and go through the following script. When you finish, put Whiskers away and out of sight.

Many Meals for Mice

PUPPET SCRIPT

Whiskers: *(Sniffing the air)* Do I smell bread? Was someone eating bread in here today? Bread is one of my favorite foods—especially if I can have it with cheese.

Teacher: Well, we did eat some bread pieces a little while ago. We went on a pretend picnic, like the one Jesus had in the Bible.

Whiskers: Oh, I love picnics! I didn't know that Jesus went on picnics, too. I like to take Swiss cheese sandwiches! What did Jesus bring?

Teacher: Your friends can tell you. Children, let's tell Whiskers how Jesus fed all the people.
   (Lead children in telling Whiskers how Jesus used one little boy's lunch of five loaves and two fish to feed the crowd.)

Whiskers: Five small loaves of bread. Hmm. Well, that's not such a big deal. Five small loaves of bread would feed my family for a whole month.

Teacher: Maybe. But do you think it would be enough for your family and Cousin Joey's family and all the other mice families on your street? Jesus fed a lot of families with just that small lunch.

Whiskers: My family and Cousin Joey's family and all the other mice families? I guess I never thought of it that way. That's amazing. And they even had leftovers? Wow! Jesus is so great. I bet ⚫Jesus can do anything.

Teacher: That's right, Whiskers. ⚫Jesus can do anything. Let's say that Point together.
   (Lead Whiskers and the children in repeating The Point.)

Whiskers: Thanks for telling me that great story. I think I'll tell it to my family at dinner tonight. Goodbye! See you next time!

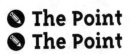

⚫ **The Point**
✏️ **The Point**

Jesus can do anything.

TODAY I LEARNED...

We believe Christian education extends beyond the classroom into the home. Photocopy the "Today I Learned..." handout (p. 120) for this week and send it home with your children. Encourage parents to use the handout to plan meaningful family activities to reinforce this week's topic. Follow up the "Today I Learned..." activities next week by asking children what their families did.

Closing

Miracle Lunch (up to 5 minutes)

Say: **Let's sing our "Miracle Lunch" song one more time to help us remember the great miracle Jesus did.**

Lead children in singing "The Miracle Lunch" with the *cassette tape*, to the tune of "Old MacDonald." As you sing, do the motions.

Sing

A little boy said, "Here, take my lunch (hold out hands, palms up);
I'm really glad to share." (Nod head.)
And with that lunch, Jesus fed the whole bunch (sweep right arm in front of you)—
Every person there. (Sweep left arm in front of you.)
With five little loaves (hold up five fingers on right hand)
And two little fish (hold up two fingers on left hand)—
Here a loaf (hold out right hand, palm up),
There a fish (hold out left hand, palm up)—
Mmm, that's a yummy dish! (Rub tummy.)
Jesus made a miracle lunch (point up to heaven)
When a little boy said, "I'll share." (Hold out both hands, palms up.)

(Repeat)

Say: ● **Jesus can do anything. Let's thank God for the great miracle Jesus did. Dear God, thank you for the great miracle Jesus did when he fed all those people. We're glad that, ● Jesus can do anything, and that he's taking care of us today. In Jesus' name, amen.**

● **The Point**
● **The Point**

Jesus can do anything.

For Extra Time

If you have a long class time or want to add additional elements to your lesson, try one of the following activities.

LIVELY LEARNING: Sing for Your Lunch

Gather children in a circle and sing this song to the tune of "Ten Little Indians." As you sing, do the motions.

Sing

One little, two little, three little loaves of bread *(hold up one finger, then two, then three),*
Three little, four little, five little loaves of bread. *(Hold up three, then four, then all five fingers.)*
Just two fish to go with our loaves of bread *(hold up two fingers on the other hand),*
But Jesus could feed us all! *(Hold both arms out with hands out-stretched.)*

MAKE TO TAKE: Lunch-Sack Baskets

Give each child a paper lunch sack. Help children cut their sacks to make baskets, as shown in the margin. Let children decorate their sack baskets with crayons, markers, or other art supplies you have on hand. Then help them open up the sacks and tape or staple the top to form a handle. As children work, remind them that Jesus' disciples collected 12 baskets of food after everyone had had enough.

TREAT TO EAT: Fishy Snack

Give each child seven fish crackers. Let children count out two crackers for the two fish and five crackers for the five loaves of bread. Before children enjoy the snack, thank God for providing it, just as he provided lunch for all the people who were listening to Jesus.

STORY PICTURE: Little Boy Shares His Lunch

Before class, cut a brown paper lunch sack into 2-inch squares. Give each child a copy of the "Today I Learned..." handout (p. 120). Let children color the picture. Set out glue and the brown paper squares you've prepared. Help children glue squares to the little boy's lunch sack in the picture. As children work, talk about how amazed the people must have been when Jesus fed the crowd with just two fish and five small loaves of bread.

Jesus can do anything.

Miracle Fish

Photocopy the handout and cut out the fish pattern.

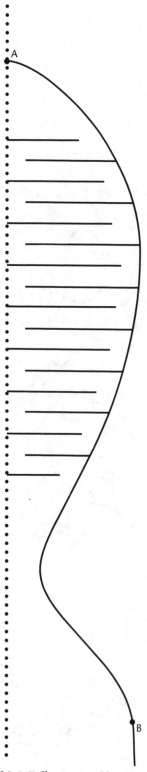

(Pattern adapted from *Clip & Tell Bible Stories,* copyright © 1995 Lois Keffer. Reprinted by permission of Group Publishing, Inc., Box 481, Loveland, CO 80539.)

Permission to photocopy this handout from Group's Hands-On Bible Curriculum™ for Preschool granted for local church use. Copyright © Group Publishing, Inc., Box 481, Loveland, CO 80539.

Jesus can do anything.

TODAY I LEARNED . . .

The Point ● Jesus can do anything.

Today your child learned that Jesus can do anything. Children heard how Jesus fed more than 5,000 people with just two fish and five small loaves of bread. They learned a song about Jesus' miracle.

Verse to Learn

"I can do all things through Christ, because he gives me strength" (Philippians 4:13).

Ask Me . . .

● What was in the little boy's lunch?

● Would you have given your lunch to Jesus to share with everyone? Explain.

● How did the people feel before Jesus fed them? How did they feel after they'd had enough to eat?

Family Fun

● Plan a family picnic. Go in your back yard, to a local park, or spread a blanket on your living room floor. Pretend you're going to hear Jesus speak. Take along your favorite lunch foods and cassette recording of your favorite Bible story to listen to while you eat your lunch.

Jesus Feeds More Than 5,000 People (John 6:1-14)

Permission to photocopy this handout from Group's Hands-On Bible Curriculum™ for Preschool granted for local church use. Copyright © Group Publishing, Inc., Box 481, Loveland, CO 80539.

LESSON 7

The Eyes Have It

The Point

✎ Jesus can do anything.

The Bible Basis

Mark 10:46-52. Jesus heals a blind man.

When Bartimaeus heard the rumble of the approaching crowd, he listened closely to see what the commotion was about. Over the clamor of conflicting conversations, his sensitive ears heard the word "Jesus" repeated again and again. Although he couldn't see Jesus, Bartimaeus knew Jesus must be in the crowd. Immediately, he began to shout out, "Jesus, Son of David, have mercy on me!" In spite of the crowd's repeated warnings to be quiet, Bartimaeus kept shouting until he gained Jesus' attention. With quiet confidence, Bartimaeus presented his request to Jesus. "Teacher, I want to see," he said. Jesus recognized Bartimaeus' sincere belief and healed him.

The 3- and 4-year-olds in your class may not have encountered a blind person. But they know how scary it is to be in the dark, and they can imagine what it might be like to be in the dark all the time. Use this lesson to teach children that Jesus can do miracles, including restoring a blind man's sight.

Getting The Point

✎ Jesus can do anything.

It's important to say The Point exactly as it's written each time it appears. Repeating The Point over and over will help the children remember it and apply it to their lives.

Children will
- discover how blind people rely on their other senses,
- hear how Jesus healed a blind man,
- experience what it might be like to be blind, and
- thank God for the gift of sight.

✎ **The Point**

This Lesson at a Glance

Before the lesson, collect the necessary items for the activities you plan to use. Refer to the Classroom Supplies and Learning Lab Supplies columns to determine what you'll need. Remember to make photocopies of the "Today I Learned..." handout (p. 132) to send home with your children.

Section	Minutes	What Children Will Do	Classroom Supplies	Learning Lab Supplies
Welcome Time	up to 5	**Welcome!**—Receive name tags and be greeted by the teacher.	"Angel Name Tags" hand-outs (p. 30)	
Let's Get Started Direct children to one or more of the Let's Get Started activities until everyone arrives.	up to 10	**Option 1: What's That Sound?**—Try to recognize familiar sounds and talk about how we use our ears to identify objects we can't see.	Cassette player	Cassette: "Familiar Sounds"
	up to 10	**Option 2: The Eyes Have It**—Make modeling dough faces with their eyes shut and hear how Jesus healed a man who couldn't see.	Paper plates, marker, modeling dough	
	up to 10	**Option 3: What's That Fruit?**—Try to identify fruit without using their eyes and hear how Jesus made a blind man see.	Lunch sacks, apple, orange, banana, grapes	
Pick-Up Song	up to 5	**Now It's Time**—Sing a song as they pick up toys and gather for Bible-Story Time.	Cassette player	Cassette: "Now It's Time"
Bible-Story Time	up to 10	**Setting the Stage**—Listen carefully for their names and hear how the blind man heard Jesus coming.		
	up to 5	**Bible Song and Prayer Time**—Sing a song, bring out the Bible, and pray together.	Bible, cassette player	Happy-face stamp and ink pad, cassette: "We Are Glad..."
	up to 5	**Hear the Bible Story**—Hear a story from Mark 10:46-52 about how Jesus healed a blind man.	Bible	Learning Mat: Jesus Can Do Anything
	up to 8	**Do the Bible Story**—Lead each other around the room as the people led the blind man to Jesus.	Chairs	
Practicing The Point	up to 8	**What Is Blind?**—Help Whiskers experience what it's like to be blind.	Whiskers the Mouse, blindfold	
Closing	up to 5	**Yes, He Can**—Sing a song and thank God for things they can see.	Cassette player	Cassette: "Yes, He Can"
For Extra Time	For extra-time ideas and supplies, see page 130.			

Jesus can do anything.

Welcome Time

Welcome! (up to 5 minutes)

- Bend down and make eye contact with children as they arrive.
- Greet each child individually with an enthusiastic smile.
- Thank each child for coming to class today.
- As children arrive, ask them about last week's "Today I Learned..." discussion. Use questions such as "What did you tell your family about the little boy who shared his lunch with Jesus?" or "Did you have a family picnic? What did you eat?"
- Say: **Today we're going to learn that**  **Jesus can do anything.**
- Hand out the angel name tags children made during Lesson 1 and help them attach the name tags to their clothing. If some of the name tags were damaged or if children weren't in class that week, have them make new name tags using the photocopiable handout on page 30.
- Direct children to the Let's Get Started activities you've set up.

● The Point

Let's Get Started

Set up one or more of the following activities for children to do as they arrive. After you greet each child, invite him or her to choose an activity.

Circulate between the activities to offer help as needed and direct children's conversation toward the point of today's lesson. Ask questions such as "What do you think it would be like if you couldn't see?" or "How did the blind man know Jesus was coming?"

☐ OPTION 1: What's That Sound? (up to 10 minutes)

Play the "Familiar Sounds" segment from the *cassette tape*. You'll hear a dog barking, footsteps, a door closing, a car horn, a cat meowing, and a baby crying. Pause the tape after you play each sound and let children guess what it is. Ask questions such as "How did you know what that was since you couldn't see it?" Explain that people who can't see with their eyes have to listen very carefully. Tell children that today's Bible story is about a time Jesus helped a blind man see.

☐ OPTION 2: The Eyes Have It (up to 10 minutes)

Before class, draw simple smiling faces (eyes and mouth only) on paper plates. Set out modeling dough and let children use the dough to add the features to their faces. Encourage them to add ears, noses, hair, and any other details they want. Have children try making the faces with their eyes shut, then have them open their eyes and see what kinds of faces they've put together. As children work, talk about how our eyes, ears, noses, mouths, and hands help us learn about the world. Point out that it's not easy to do things when we can't see. Explain that today's Bible story is about a time Jesus helped a blind man see.

Jesus can do anything.

☐ Option 3: What's That Fruit? (up to 10 minutes)

In separate paper lunch sacks, place an apple, an orange, a banana, and a bunch of grapes. Let children try to identify the fruit in each bag first by smelling and then by touching. Talk about what it would be like to be blind and have to identify some things by only touch and smell. Explain that today's Bible story is about a blind man who asked Jesus to help him see.

After everyone's had a chance to guess, reveal the contents of each bag. You may want to cut up the fruit and let children sample each one.

When everyone has arrived and you're ready to move on to Bible-Story Time, encourage the children to finish what they're doing and get ready to clean up.

Pick-Up Song

Now It's Time (up to 5 minutes)

Lead children in singing "Now It's Time" with the *cassette tape*, to the tune of "The Mulberry Bush." Encourage children to sing along as they help clean up the room.

Sing

Now it's time to clean up our room,
Clean up our room,
Clean up our room.
Now it's time to clean up our room
And put our things away.

Will you help me? Yes, I will.
Yes, I will.
Yes, I will!
Will you help me? Yes, I will.
I'll help you right away.

(Repeat)

Bible-Story Time

Setting the Stage (up to 10 minutes)

Tell the children you'll clap your hands three times to get their attention. Explain that when you clap your hands, the children are to stop what they're doing and repeat the clap. Practice this signal a few times. Encourage children to respond quickly so you'll have time for all the fun activities you've planned. Ask:

● **What did you make or do when you came to our class today?** (Listened to sounds; made a face with dough; guessed what kind of fruit was in the bags.)

Say: **If you made a face with modeling dough, stand up and show me a funny face you can make, then sit down.** Pause. **If you tried to guess which kind of fruit was in the bags, raise your hand and tell me your favorite fruit to eat.** Pause. **If you listened to sounds, stand up and make**

Jesus can do anything.

one of the sounds you heard, then sit down. Pause.

Say: **You've all been learning how important our eyesight is to us. People who can't see have to use their senses of touch, taste, smell, and hearing to discover things. Let's play a game now where we use our hearing to discover who's calling us.**

Have children sit in a circle on the floor. Choose one child to sit in the center. Say: (Name of child in the center), **in just a minute I'm going to have you close your eyes. While your eyes are closed, I'll ask someone else in our circle to say your name. Without opening your eyes, when you hear your name, point to the person who's calling you and say his or her name if you know it.**

Have the child sitting in the center close his or her eyes, then choose another child to call out the center child's name. Let the child in the center guess who called his or her name and then join the circle. Continue until everyone has had a turn in the center. Then ask:

● **What was it like to guess who was calling you without looking?** (Hard; fun; I couldn't guess.)

Say: **It's fun to close our eyes and play a game. Today we'll hear about a man who couldn't see anything even when his eyes were open. He was blind, but he knew that Jesus could help him.** ✎**Jesus can do anything, even make a blind man see. Let's bring out our Bible and get ready for that story now.**

● **The Point**

Bible Song and Prayer Time (up to 5 minutes)

Say: **Now it's time to choose a Bible person to bring me the Bible marked with today's Bible story. As we sing our Bible song, we'll pass around our special Bible. The person who's holding the Bible when the music stops will be our Bible person today.**

Lead children in singing "We Are Glad to Read the Bible" with the *cassette tape,* to the tune of "Did You Ever See a Lassie?" As you sing, pass around the special Bible.

Sing

We are glad to read the Bible,
The Bible, the Bible.
We are glad to read the Bible
For it is God's Book.

We'll hear Bible stories
And learn about God's love.
We are glad to read the Bible
For it is God's Book.

When the music stops, invite the child who's holding the Bible to bring it to you. Stamp the child's hand with the *happy-face stamp* and thank him or her for bringing you the Bible. Then stamp the other children's hands. Return the *happy-face stamp and ink pad* to the Learning Lab.

Say: **I'm thankful for** (name of child who brought the Bible) **and I'm thankful for everyone in our class today. Let's thank God together for all our friends in this class.**

Lead children in singing "We Are Glad to Pray Together" to the tune of "Did You Ever See a Lassie?" If you want to include the names of all the children in your class, sing the song without the cassette and repeat the naming section. If you choose to use the cassette, vary the names you use each week.

Jesus can do anything.

Sing

We are glad to pray together,
Together, together.
We are glad to pray together
And give thanks to God.

Lead children in folding their
hands and bowing their heads as
you continue to sing.

Thank you for (name),
And (name), and (name).
Thank you, God, for every person
Who's here in our class.

(Repeat)

Hear the Bible Story (up to 5 minutes)

Gather the children around the *Learning Mat: Jesus Can Do Anything*. Open the Bible to Mark 10:46-52 and show it to the children. Say: **Our story comes from the book of Mark in the Bible, God's special book. Our *Learning Mat* shows us pictures of our Bible story.**

Say: **We're going to hear about a blind man who called out to Jesus. Some people thought the blind man would bother Jesus, so they told him to stop calling and be quiet. I want you to listen very carefully to our Bible story. Every time you hear me say, "blind man," put your finger over your mouth and say "Shhh!" Let's try that. Blind man.**

Pause for children to say "Shhh!" then continue: **At the end of our story we'll shout "Hurray!" together. Let's try that. Hurray!**

Say: **One day Jesus was walking to the town of Jericho. A <u>blind man</u> named Bartimaeus was sitting by the side of the road. Can you find the <u>blind man</u> on our *Learning Mat*?**

Pause and help children find the blind man on the *Learning Mat,* then continue: **The <u>blind man</u> heard a crowd of people coming, and he heard that Jesus was in the crowd. The <u>blind man</u> got very excited when he heard that Jesus was coming because he knew that Jesus could help him see.**

The <u>blind man</u> called out, "Jesus, have mercy on me!" That meant he wanted Jesus to be kind to him and help him see. The <u>blind man</u> wanted to make sure Jesus would hear, so he shouted as loud as he could. The people in the crowd thought the <u>blind man</u> would bother Jesus. They told the <u>blind man</u> to be quiet. Do you think the <u>blind man</u> would bother Jesus? Let children respond.

✎ The Point

The <u>blind man</u> knew that ⬤ Jesus can do anything. He shouted even louder, "Jesus, have mercy on me!" Well, Jesus heard the <u>blind man</u> calling him. He said, "Tell the man to come here."

The people in the crowd called the <u>blind man</u>. They said, "Cheer up! Jesus is calling you!" So the <u>blind man</u> jumped up right away and walked over to Jesus.

Jesus asked the <u>blind man</u>, "What do you want me to do for you?" The <u>blind man</u> answered Jesus, "I want to see." Jesus could tell that the <u>blind man</u> believed in him. Jesus said, "You are healed because you believed in me." And right away the <u>blind man</u> could see! Let's see what happened after Jesus healed him.

Open the window on the *Learning Mat* to reveal the blind man standing up, ready to follow Jesus. Say: **The man followed Jesus down the road.**

When I count to three, let's all stand up and shout "Hurray!" for Jesus and his mighty power. One, two, three—hurray!

Now let's play a game to help us see what it was like for the blind man before Jesus healed him.

Do the Bible Story (up to 8 minutes)

Set up a short obstacle course with a couple of chairs. Form pairs. Say: **Let's see what it might have been like for Bartimaeus when he was blind. One partner will close his or her eyes and pretend to be blind. The other partner will keep his or her eyes open and lead the blind partner around the chairs. Then we'll switch and the other partner can pretend to be blind. I'd like the person who's wearing the most red to be the blind partner first.**

Have partners line up and lead each other around the chairs. Remind "seeing" partners to be careful as they guide their "blind" partners. After everyone has walked around the chairs, let children switch roles and repeat the activity. Then gather children in your story area. Ask:

● **What was it like to be the blind partner?** (Hard to keep my eyes closed; scary; I peeked.)

● **What was it like to be the partner who could see?** (I had to be careful; it was fun.)

Say: **The blind man in our Bible story always needed someone to help him, just as you needed your partners to guide you around the chairs. He wanted to see so he could walk around by himself and look at all the beautiful things God has made. He knew that ⬤Jesus can do anything. That's why he asked Jesus to help him see.**

You know, I bet our friend Whiskers would like to hear our story about the blind man. Let's close our eyes and quietly call for him.

Lead children in calling for Whiskers.

⬤ The Point

✔ If you have a large class, you may want to set up more than one obstacle course so that more than one set of children can be participating at one time.

Practicing The Point

What Is Blind? (up to 8 minutes)

Bring out Whiskers and a blindfold and go through the following script. When you finish the script, put Whiskers away and out of sight.

Jesus can do anything.

What Is Blind?

PUPPET SCRIPT

Whiskers: Hi, friends. Have you heard any good Bible stories today?

Teacher: Of course, Whiskers. We hear a Bible story every time we come to this class.

Whiskers: Well, what happened in the story? Tell me, tell me, please!

Teacher: Children, let's tell Whiskers how Jesus healed the blind man in our story.

(Help children begin to tell Whiskers the story, then have Whiskers interrupt.)

Whiskers: Hold it, hold it. I don't understand. What does blind mean?

Teacher: Can someone tell Whiskers what it means to be blind?

(Help children explain that blind people can't see.)

Whiskers: We mice can't see very well either—that's why I sometimes have to wear glasses. Did he try getting glasses?

Teacher: Most blind people can't see anything at all, even with glasses. That's why it's so amazing that Jesus helped the man see.

Whiskers: I wonder what it would be like to be blind.

Teacher: We just played a game to help us see what it might be like to be blind. Would you like to try it?

Whiskers: *(Sounding suspicious)* What do I have to do?

Teacher: We'll cover your eyes, then your friends will lead you across the room.

Whiskers: OK, I'll try it.

(Put the blindfold over Whiskers' eyes and have children help you lead him across the room.)

Whiskers: Be careful now—I can't see anything. Don't let me trip and fall.

(When you reach the other side of the room, remove Whiskers' blindfold.)

Teacher: See, Whiskers, your friends didn't let you down. You trusted us! The man in our story had to trust the people in the crowd to help him find the way to Jesus.

Whiskers: And Jesus helped him see! That's really great. ✏ Jesus really can do anything. Let's close our eyes and say that together. Jesus can do anything. Now let's say it with our eyes open, like the blind man after Jesus helped him see. Jesus can do anything!

(Continued)

🖊 **The Point**

Jesus can do anything.

Teacher: Thanks for coming to visit us, Whiskers.

Whiskers: You bet! I love hearing about all the great things Jesus can do. I'll see you next week—I hope you'll have another Bible story for me. Goodbye!

TODAY I LEARNED...

We believe Christian education extends beyond the classroom into the home. Photocopy the "Today I Learned..." handout (p. 132) for this week and send it home with your children. Encourage parents to use the handout to plan meaningful family activities to reinforce this week's topic. Follow up the "Today I Learned..." activities next week by asking children what their families did.

Closing

Yes, He Can (up to 5 minutes)

Say: ⬤ **Jesus can do anything. Let's sing a song about that.**

Lead children in singing "Yes, He Can" with the *cassette tape,* to the tune of "London Bridge." The song is recorded on the cassette twice.

⬤ **The Point**

Sing

Jesus can do anything!
Yes, he can! Clap your hands!
Jesus can do anything!
Yes, he can!

Jesus can do miracles!
Yes, he can! Clap your hands!
Jesus can do miracles!
Yes, he can!

Gather the children in a circle and have everyone hold hands. Say: **Before we say a prayer, let's use our eyes and look around our room. What do you see that you can be thankful for?** (Toys; the Bible; other children.)

Say: **Now let's all close our eyes and pray together. Dear God, thank you for giving us eyesight to see all the beautiful things you've made. In Jesus' name, amen.**

For Extra Time

If you have a long class time or want to add additional elements to your lesson, try one of the following activities.

LIVELY LEARNING: Cheer Up!

Have children sit in a circle and choose one child to be "It." Review how Jesus healed the blind man, then have children in the circle bow their heads and cover their eyes as if they were blind. Have It tap children on the head and say, "Be quiet." When It taps a child and says, "Cheer up! Jesus is calling you!" that child must jump up and give It a hug. Then that child is It. Continue the game until everyone has had a turn to be It.

MAKE TO TAKE: Eyes That See

Photocopy the "Eyes That See" handout on page 131. You'll need a handout and a 1×10-inch white paper strip for each child.

Set out crayons and let children color the face on the handout. As they're coloring, cut the slits on each child's handout as marked. Then pass out the paper strips and have children draw open eyes on one side of the strip and closed eyes on the other side. Show children how to slide the strips through the slits. Encourage them to use their faces to retell the story of how Jesus healed the blind man. Remind them that ● Jesus can do anything.

● **The Point**

TREAT TO EAT: Cracker Eyes

Set out round crackers, spreadable cream cheese, plastic knives, and raisins. Help each child spread cream cheese on two crackers and then add raisins to create cracker eyes. Thank God for the snack and for the gift of sight, then enjoy! As children eat, review how Jesus helped the blind man see.

STORY PICTURE: Jesus Heals a Blind Man

Give each child a copy of the "Today I Learned..." handout (p. 132). Set out crayons or markers and let children color the picture. Then set out colored facial tissue and glue and help the children glue the facial tissue to the blind man's coat in the picture. Point out that the man jumped up and left his coat when he went to Jesus. Remind children that ● Jesus can do anything.

● **The Point**

Jesus can do anything.

Eyes That See

Photocopy the handout. You'll need one handout for each child.

Permission to photocopy this handout from Group's Hands-On Bible Curriculum™ for Preschool granted for local church use.
Copyright © Group Publishing, Inc., Box 481, Loveland, CO 80539.

TODAY I LEARNED . . .

The Point ● Jesus can do anything.

Today your child learned that Jesus can do anything. Children heard how Jesus healed a blind man. They did activities to see what it might be like to be blind and thanked God for the gift of sight.

Verse to Learn

"I can do all things through Christ, because he gives me strength" (Philippians 4:13).

Ask Me . . .

● Why was the blind man shouting?
● Why were people telling the blind man to be quiet?
● What did the blind man do when he found out Jesus was calling him?

Family Fun

● Sing this song with your child, to the tune of "London Bridge."

Jesus can do anything!
Yes, he can! Clap your hands!
Jesus can do anything!
Yes, he can!

(Repeat)

Jesus Heals a Blind Man (Mark 10:46-52)

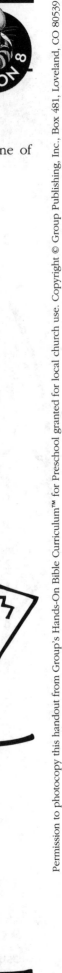
Permission to photocopy this handout from Group's Hands-On Bible Curriculum™ for Preschool granted for local church use. Copyright © Group Publishing, Inc., Box 481, Loveland, CO 80539.

Cast Out Your Net

The Point
✎ Jesus can do anything.

The Bible Basis

John 21:1-13. A miraculous catch of fish.

After Jesus' death and resurrection, his followers returned to their fishing boats. When Peter declared, "I'm going out to fish," six other followers joined him. These experienced fishermen fished all night but caught nothing. They must have laughed when a man, who first appeared to be a stranger, suggested they try casting their nets on the other side of the boat. But when the nets quickly filled with fish, one disciple recognized the risen Lord. Quickly, Peter jumped into the water and swam to shore where Jesus was waiting with a breakfast of fish and bread. The other followers brought in the boat, dragging the bulging net along in the water.

Young children are fascinated by fish, so they'll love this story about the flipping, flopping fish that filled the disciples' net. Just as the disciples were excited to discover Jesus standing on the shore, preschoolers will delight in hearing about Jesus' miracle. Use this lesson to reinforce again that Jesus can do anything.

Getting The Point

✎ Jesus can do anything.

It's important to say The Point exactly as it's written each time it appears. Repeating The Point over and over will help the children remember it and apply it to their lives.

Children will
- play fishing games,
- hear about the disciples' miraculous catch of fish,
- pretend to go fishing with the disciples, and
- fill a net with "fish" prayers as they name things they're thankful for.

● **The Point**

This Lesson at a Glance

Before the lesson, collect the necessary items for the activities you plan to use. Refer to the Classroom Supplies and Learning Lab Supplies columns to determine what you'll need. Remember to make photocopies of the "Today I Learned..." handout (p. 143) to send home with your children.

Section	Minutes	What Children Will Do	Classroom Supplies	Learning Lab Supplies
Welcome Time	up to 5	**Welcome!**—Receive name tags and be greeted by the teacher.	"Angel Name Tags" handouts (p. 30)	
Let's Get Started Direct children to one or more of the Let's Get Started activities until everyone arrives.	up to 12	**Option 1: Heart Fish**—Make heart-shaped fish and hear how Jesus' followers went fishing.	Heart-shaped cutouts, crayons or markers	
	up to 12	**Option 2: Let's Go Fishing**—"Fish" for beans and hear about a time Jesus' followers went fishing.	Dry beans, shallow tub of water, paper cups, towel	
	up to 12	**Option 3: Net Full of Fish**—Fill a blanket "net" with toy "fish" and hear how the disciples' net was full of fish.	Blanket, toys	
Pick-Up Song	up to 5	**Now It's Time**—Sing a song as they pick up toys and gather for Bible-Story Time.	Cassette player	Cassette: "Now It's Time"
Bible-Story Time	up to 8	**Setting the Stage**—Pretend to be the fish that swam into the disciples' net.		Paper net
	up to 5	**Bible Song and Prayer Time**—Sing a song, bring out the Bible, and pray together.	Bible, cassette player	Happy-face stamp and ink pad, cassette: "We Are Glad..."
	up to 8	**Hear the Bible Story**—Hear how Jesus helped his followers fill their net with fish.	Bible, cassette player	Learning Mat: Jesus Can Do Anything, cassette: "Night Fishing," "Yes, He Can"
	up to 5	**Do the Bible Story**—Do an action rhyme to review the Bible story.		
Practicing The Point	up to 8	**Fish-Net Tangle**—Tell Whiskers about the disciples' net full of fish.	Whiskers the Mouse	Paper net
Closing	up to 5	**Net Full of Prayers**—Fill a net with fish as they share things they're thankful for.	Heart fish from Option 1	Paper net
For Extra Time		For extra-time ideas and supplies, see page 142.		

Jesus can do anything.

Welcome Time

Welcome! (up to 5 minutes)

- Bend down and make eye contact with children as they arrive.
- Greet each child individually with an enthusiastic smile.
- Thank each child for coming to class today.
- As children arrive, ask them about last week's "Today I Learned . . ." discussion. Use questions such as "What did you tell your family about the blind man?" or "How did the blind man get Jesus' attention?"
- Say: **Today we're going to learn that ⬤Jesus can do anything.**
- Hand out the angel name tags children made during Lesson 1 and help them attach the name tags to their clothing. If some of the name tags were damaged or if children weren't in class that week, have them make new name tags using the photocopiable handout on page 30.
- Direct children to the Let's Get Started activities you've set up.

⬤ **The Point**

Let's Get Started

Set up one or more of the following activities for children to do as they arrive. After you greet each child, invite him or her to choose an activity.

Circulate among the children to offer help as needed and direct children's conversation toward the point of today's lesson. Ask questions such as "Have you ever been fishing? Tell me about it" or "How many fish do you think you could catch in one day?"

OPTION 1: Heart Fish (up to 12 minutes)

Before class, cut 2- and 4-inch hearts from colored construction paper. You'll need one 2-inch heart and one 4-inch heart for each child.

Give each child a small heart and a large heart. Show children how to make fish by gluing the hearts together at the points. Point out that the larger heart is the fish's head and body, and the smaller heart is its tail. Set out crayons and let children draw fins and scales on their fish. As they work, tell them that today's Bible story is about a time when Jesus' followers went fishing.

If children finish their fish early, have them make another fish to share. You'll need one fish for each child in your class. You'll use the fish later in the lesson.

OPTION 2: Let's Go Fishing (up to 12 minutes)

Empty a package of dry beans into a shallow tub of water. Let children "go fishing" with paper cups to see how many bean "fish" they can catch. Encourage them to count the beans in their cups each time and then empty their cups and try to catch more. As children fish, tell them that today's Bible story is about Jesus' disciples going fishing. Explain that the disciples didn't catch anything at first, but then Jesus told them how to fill their nets with fish. Remind children that ⬤Jesus can do anything.

Have a towel available for children to dry their hands on when they finish fishing.

⬤ **The Point**

OPTION 3: Net Full of Fish (up to 12 minutes)

Lay a blanket on the floor. Invite children to place classroom toys or blocks in the center of the blanket, then pull the edges of the blanket together. Let children take turns dragging the blanket around the room. Encourage them to try it by themselves, with partners, and then all together. Explain that today's Bible story is about a time Jesus' disciples dragged a heavy net full of fish. Point out that Jesus helped the disciples catch the fish and remind children that Jesus can do anything.

● The Point

> ✔ If you have a knitted or crocheted afghan, bring it in for this activity. With its pattern of holes, an afghan will seem even more net-like.

When everyone has arrived and you're ready to move on to Bible-Story Time, encourage the children to finish what they're doing and get ready to clean up.

Pick-Up Song

Now It's Time (up to 5 minutes)

Lead children in singing "Now It's Time" with the *cassette tape,* to the tune of "The Mulberry Bush." Encourage children to sing along as they help clean up the room.

Sing

Now it's time to clean up our room,
Clean up our room,
Clean up our room.
Now it's time to clean up our room
And put our things away.

Will you help me? Yes, I will.
Yes, I will.
Yes, I will!
Will you help me? Yes, I will.
I'll help you right away.

(Repeat)

Bible-Story Time

Setting the Stage (up to 8 minutes)

If you did the "Net Full of Fish" activity during Let's Get Started, spread out the blanket to create a pretend beach for children to sit on during Bible-Story Time.

Tell the children you'll clap your hands three times to get their attention. Explain that when you clap your hands, the children are to stop what they're doing and repeat the clap. Practice this signal a few times. Encourage children to respond quickly so you'll have time for all the fun activities you've planned. Ask:

Jesus can do anything.

● **What did you make or do when you came to our class today?** (Made a fish out of hearts; went fishing in the water; dragged the net.)

Say: **Some of you made heart fish, some of you went fishing for beans, and some of you dragged a pretend net around our room. You were all learning important things about our Bible story. Today's Bible story is about a time some of Jesus' disciples went fishing.** Ask:

● **Have you ever been fishing? Tell us about it.** (I went with my grandpa; we had to get up early; we had to use worms to catch the fish.)

● **What did you use to fish with?** (A fishing pole; worms; a net.)

Hold up the *paper net.* Say: **When Jesus' disciples went fishing, they used a net. Their net was sort of like this one, but it was much, much bigger. They would throw their net out into the sea and wait for the fish to swim into it—just like this.**

Gently throw the *paper net* out over the children. Say: **Oh my! You're the biggest fish I've ever seen. If I tried to catch all of you, my net would break for sure.**

Have children pass the net back to you. Say: **Let's play a game with our net to help us get ready for our Bible story. A few of us will hold the net up high over our heads.**

Choose three or four children to help you hold up the net, then continue: **The rest of you will be fish. You'll swim under the net, one at a time, and we'll try to drop the net down and catch you. When you get caught, you must swim over to our story area and pretend to flop down in the boat.**

Let children take turns "swimming" under the net. You'll probably be able to catch most of them on the first try. As children get caught, have them go sit in the story area. If your net holders want to get caught, invite a few children from the story area to help hold the net. When everyone's been caught, return the *paper net* to the Learning Lab and join children in the story area.

Say: **That was fun! When Jesus' disciples went fishing, they did what Jesus said, and their net filled with fish. ◖Jesus can do anything. Let's bring out our Bible and hear how Jesus helped his friends catch fish.**

● **The Point**

Bible Song and Prayer Time (up to 5 minutes)

Say: **Now it's time to choose a Bible person to bring me the Bible marked with today's Bible story. As we sing our Bible song, we'll pass around our special Bible. The person who's holding the Bible when the music stops will be our Bible person today.**

Lead children in singing "We Are Glad to Read the Bible" with the *cassette tape,* to the tune of "Did You Ever See a Lassie?" As you sing, pass around the special Bible.

Sing

We are glad to read the Bible,
The Bible, the Bible.
We are glad to read the Bible
For it is God's Book.

We'll hear Bible stories
And learn about God's love.
We are glad to read the Bible
For it is God's Book.

When the music stops, invite the child who's holding the Bible to bring it to you. Stamp the child's hand with the *happy-face stamp* and thank him or her for bringing you the Bible. Then stamp the other children's hands. Return the *happy-face stamp and ink pad* to the Learning Lab.

Say: **I'm thankful for** (name of child who brought the Bible) **and I'm thankful for everyone in our class today. Let's thank God together for all our friends in this class.**

Lead children in singing "We Are Glad to Pray Together" to the tune of "Did You Ever See a Lassie?" If you want to include the names of all the children in your class, sing the song without the cassette and repeat the naming section. If you choose to use the cassette, vary the names you use each week.

Sing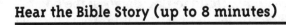

We are glad to pray together,
Together, together.
We are glad to pray together
And give thanks to God.

Lead children in folding their hands and bowing their heads as you continue to sing.

Thank you for (name),
And (name), **and** (name).
Thank you, God, for every person
Who's here in our class.

(Repeat)

Hear the Bible Story (up to 8 minutes)

Gather the children around the *Learning Mat: Jesus Can Do Anything.* Open the Bible to John 21:1-13 and show it to the children. Say: **Our story comes from the book of John in the Bible, God's special book. Our *Learning Mat* shows us pictures of our Bible story.**

Listen carefully to our story today. Every time you hear the word "fish" or "fishing" on the tape, pretend to cast out your net. Let's practice that. Fishing.

Let children practice casting pretend nets, then play the "Night Fishing" segment from the *cassette tape.* Follow along in the text below so you can help children remember to cast out their nets.

"I'm going <u>fishing</u>," Peter said as he looked out over the water. "It looks like a good night to go <u>fishing</u>."

Peter's friends decided to go with him. So they all got into Peter's boat and went out to <u>fish</u> on the lake. They rowed the boat out into the water, then they threw out their nets and waited for the <u>fish</u> to swim right in. They waited, and waited, and waited. But every time Peter and his friends pulled their nets out of the water, they were empty!

Peter and his friends kept <u>fishing</u> all night long, but they didn't catch a single <u>fish</u>. They were discouraged and very, very tired. Early in the morning, when the sun was just beginning to peek over the edge of the water, they saw a man standing on the shore.

"Friends, did you catch any <u>fish</u>?" the man called out.

Peter and his friends shook their heads sadly. "No," they called back.

"Throw your net on the right side of the boat, and you will find some <u>fish</u>," the man said.

Peter and his friends weren't sure about that. They hadn't seen a single <u>fish</u>

all night. But they did what the man said. Right away, their net filled with <u>fish</u>. Slippery, flippery, <u>fish</u>. Big <u>fish</u>, little <u>fish</u>, scaly <u>fish</u>, slimy <u>fish</u>. The net was so full of <u>fish</u> that Peter and his friends couldn't even pull it back into the boat.

One of Peter's friends looked at the man on the shore again. "It's Jesus!" he shouted. ●Jesus can do anything, and he had helped his friends fill their net with <u>fish</u>.

Right away, Peter jumped out of the boat and started swimming back to shore. The rest of the friends stayed in the boat and rowed back to shore, dragging the net full of <u>fish</u> behind them.

When they got to the shore, Jesus was waiting. He asked them to have breakfast with him. And do you know what they ate for breakfast? Some of the <u>fish</u> they'd caught! They were glad to be with their friend Jesus once more.

● **The Point**

After the story, stop the tape and open the window on the *Learning Mat* to reveal the disciples' net full of fish. Say: **Look at all the fish in the net!** ●**Jesus really can do anything! Let's sing a song to celebrate Jesus' great miracles.**

● **The Point**

Lead the children in singing "Yes, He Can" with the *cassette tape,* to the tune of "London Bridge."

Sing

Jesus can do anything!	**Jesus can do miracles!**
Yes, he can! Clap your hands!	**Yes, he can! Clap your hands!**
Jesus can do anything!	**Jesus can do miracles!**
Yes, he can!	**Yes, he can!**

Do the Bible Story (up to 5 minutes)

Say: ●**Jesus can do anything. Let's do an action rhyme to help us remember how he helped his disciples fill their net with fish. I'll say the words, and you can do the motions with me.**

● **The Point**

Lead children in the following action rhyme. As you say each line, do the motions.

Seven disciples went out to fish *(hold up seven fingers)*
Across the wet sand, squishety-squish. *(Walk in place.)*
They rowed their boat in the fading light. *(Make rowing motions.)*
They planned to fish very late that night. *(Wiggle hands like fish swimming.)*
Into the water they cast their net *(pretend to throw out net)*
To see how many fish they'd get. *(Wiggle hands like fish swimming.)*
All night they fished without a sound. *(Cup hands around ears.)*
There simply were no fish around! *(Shake head.)*
Then someone said, "Try once again. *(Hold up one finger.)*
Cast on the other side, and then *(pretend to cast net)*
Your net will fill right up with fish. *(Hold out arms to indicate a full net.)*
We'll eat them for a breakfast dish." *(Pretend to eat.)*
They cast their net out to the right *(pretend to cast net)*,
Then flip-flop, flip-flop—what a sight! *(Wiggle hands like fish swimming.)*
One fish swam in, then more and more. *(Make swimming motions.)*
It must be Jesus on the shore! *(Nod head and point up to heaven.)*

Jesus can do anything.

If children enjoy the rhyme, you may want to repeat it so they can learn to say the words with you.

Say: **It was Jesus on the shore, wasn't it? Do you think our friend Whiskers would like to hear that story? I know he likes to go camping—maybe he likes fishing, too. Let's call him.**

Lead children in calling for Whiskers.

Practicing The Point

Fish-Net Tangle (up to 8 minutes)

Bring out Whiskers, all tangled up in the *paper net*, and go through the following script. When you finish the script, put Whiskers away. Keep the *paper net* on hand to use during the closing activity.

Fish-Net Tangle

PUPPET SCRIPT

Whiskers: Hello, friends! I'm really glad to see you today. Could someone please untangle me?

Teacher: Sure. We'll help you. *(Invite a child to help you untangle Whiskers from the net.)* Where did you get this net, Whiskers?

Whiskers: My mom and I got it at a garage sale. The man there said I could go fishing with it. But I'm not sure about that. I've been fishing, and this thing sure doesn't look like a fishing pole to me.

Teacher: It's not a fishing pole, Whiskers. It's a fishing net. We just heard a Bible story about some of Jesus' friends who went fishing with a fishing net. Maybe some of your friends here could show you how Jesus' friends used their nets for fishing.

Whiskers: Yes! Would you please?

(Invite children to make casting motions, then take the net from Whiskers and cast it aside, out of children's reach.)

Whiskers: Wow! That's neat. What happened when Jesus' friends went fishing with their nets? Did they catch anything? I never seem to catch anything when I go fishing.

(Let children respond. Help them tell Whiskers that at first the disciples caught nothing. But as soon as Jesus told them where to cast their net, the net filled with fish.)

 **The Point**

Teacher: ◗ Jesus can do anything. The disciples didn't catch any fish all night, but when Jesus told them what to do, their net filled up right away!

Whiskers: That's great. Jesus really can do anything. He helped people who were sick, he fed all those people with fish and bread, and now he filled his friends' net with fish.

(Continued)

Jesus can do anything.

Teacher: Jesus loves us very much, and he can help us, just as he helped the people in our Bible stories.

Whiskers: I love hearing Bible stories. And you know what? I tell Cousin Joey about them, too. Maybe Cousin Joey and I can use my net to go fishing in his bathtub. Then I can tell him about Jesus' friends and the net full of fish. Goodbye! See you next week.

TODAY I LEARNED . . .

We believe Christian education extends beyond the classroom into the home. Photocopy the "Today I Learned . . ." handout (p. 143) for this week and send it home with your children. Encourage parents to use the handout to plan meaningful family activities to reinforce this week's topic. Follow up the "Today I Learned . . ." activities next week by asking children what their families did.

Closing

Net Full of Prayers (up to 5 minutes)

Gather the children in a circle and say: **We've been learning that 🖊 Jesus can do anything. He made sick people well, fed over 5,000 people, and helped his disciples catch a net full of fish. Isn't it great that Jesus loves us so much and wants to do all these wonderful things for us? Let's use our fish net to say a thank you prayer to Jesus.**

Spread out the *paper net* on the floor and hand each child a heart fish from Option 1. Make sure children who made fish get their own. Have children sit around the outside of the net.

Say: **We're going to go around the circle and take turns dropping our fish into the net. As you drop your fish, say one thing you'd like to thank Jesus for. You might choose something from one of our Bible stories. For example, you could say, "Thank you for healing sick people" or "Thank you for the net full of fish." Or you might choose something else you're thankful for such as your family, your house, or your friends. I'll go first.**

Drop your fish into the net on the floor and say something you're thankful for. If some children can't think of anything, encourage them to place their fish in the net and simply say, "Thank you, Jesus."

When all the fish are in the net, close with a prayer similar to this one: **Dear Jesus, we know that you can do anything. Thanks for all the great things you do for us today. Amen.**

🖊 The Point

Jesus can do anything.

For Extra Time

If you have a long class time or want to add additional elements to your lesson, try one of the following activities.

LIVELY LEARNING: *Learning Mat Review*

Set out the *Learning Mat: Jesus Can Do Anything*. Let children open and close the windows on the mat to reveal "before" and "after" scenes from the miracles they've been learning about. Encourage them to ask each other what's under each window. They can also use the mat to retell the stories to Whiskers. As they interact with the stories, remind them that  Jesus can do anything.

MAKE TO TAKE: **Fish Nets**

Before class, cut colored yarn into 8-inch lengths. Mix equal parts of water and white glue in a bowl.

Give each child a sheet of blue construction paper and several lengths of yarn. Show each child how to dip the yarn into the glue mixture and then arrange the yarn on the paper to look like a fishing net. Let them glue fish crackers or extra heart fish from Let's Get Started in their nets. As they work, talk about how Jesus filled the disciples' net after they'd been fishing all night. Remind children that ●Jesus can do anything.

TREAT TO EAT: **Fisherman's Breakfast**

Remind children that after Jesus helped Peter and his friends catch so many fish, they had a special fish breakfast together. Set out bowls of tuna fish, plastic knives, and crackers. Let children fix themselves crackers and tuna fish, thank God for the great miracle Jesus did, and then enjoy their snacks.

STORY PICTURE: **The Miraculous Catch**

Give each child a copy of the "Today I Learned..." handout (p. 143). Set out crayons and let children color their pictures. Then set out fish crackers and glue. Help children glue the fish crackers on the net in the picture. As children work, review how Jesus filled his disciples' net with fish. Remind children that ●Jesus can do anything.

● **The Point**

Jesus can do anything.

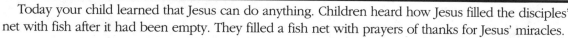

TODAY I LEARNED . . .

The Point ● Jesus can do anything.

Today your child learned that Jesus can do anything. Children heard how Jesus filled the disciples' net with fish after it had been empty. They filled a fish net with prayers of thanks for Jesus' miracles.

Verse to Learn

"I can do all things through Christ, because he gives me strength" (Philippians 4:13).

Ask Me . . .

● What did Jesus tell the disciples to do with their net?

● What happened when the disciples did what Jesus asked?

● What's your favorite Bible story about Jesus' miracles?

Family Fun

● Fill a sink or dishpan with water and let your child use a colander to fish for gummy fish (or gummy worms if fish aren't available). As you're fishing, ask your child to tell you how Jesus filled his disciples' net with fish. Eat the gummy fish you catch!

The Miraculous Catch of Fish (John 21:1-13)

Permission to photocopy this handout from Group's Hands-On Bible Curriculum™ for Preschool granted for local church use. Copyright © Group Publishing, Inc., Box 481, Loveland, CO 80539.

Zacchaeus

Zacchaeus was a sly entrepreneur who collected more taxes than the hated Roman government required and then pocketed the surplus. His dishonest business dealings made him a wealthy—and despised—man. Since the people of Jericho considered Zacchaeus a thief and a traitor, they must have been shocked when Jesus invited himself to Zacchaeus' home. But Jesus' unconditional love softened Zacchaeus' sin-hardened heart and dramatically changed his life. That very day Jesus announced that salvation had come to Zacchaeus' house.

Just like the people of Jericho, preschoolers learn by example. We often hear them use adult phrases, mimic our phone conversations, or treat others as they are treated. It's our responsibility to give children a loving, accepting example just as Jesus did. The lessons in this module will provide opportunities for children to give and receive love and kindness.

Four Lessons on Zacchaeus

	Page	The Point	Bible Basis
Lesson 10 **Seeing Is Believing**	149	Jesus wants us to love him.	Luke 19:1-4
Lesson 11 **A Kind Invitation**	159	Jesus wants us to be kind.	Luke 19:5-7
Lesson 12 **Sincerely Sorry**	169	Jesus wants us to be sorry when we do wrong.	Luke 19:8
Lesson 13 **Doin' It Right**	181	Jesus wants us to do what's right.	Luke 19:9-10

Time Stretchers

Give It Away

Mark a tape line in your room. Place a bowl of treats on each side of the line.

Form two groups and send each group to a different side of the line. Say: **To show how much he loved Jesus, Zacchaeus gave half of his money away. In this game, your group will try to give all your treats to the other group. The other group will try to give their treats away, too! Let's see if you can give away all your treats in one minute.**

On your signal, have children walk to the bowls, take one treat, hop to the other group's bowl, and set the treat inside. Call time after one minute. Show children that neither bowl is empty! Explain that when we give our best to Jesus, he give us good things in return. Give each child a treat to enjoy.

Treetop Singers

Teach children "See Zacchaeus," to the tune of "The Mulberry Bush."

Sing

**See Zacchaeus climb a tree,
Climb a tree, climb a tree.** (*Do climbing motions.*)
**See Zacchaeus climb up a tree.
Now tell me what you see.** (*Put hand over eyes, searching.*)

**I see Jesus walking by,
Walking by, walking by.** (*Walk in a circle.*)
**I see Jesus walking by.
He sees me here, up high.** (*Look up and point.*)

**Look! Now Jesus is calling me,
Calling me, calling me.** (*Cup hands to mouth.*)

**Look! Now Jesus is calling me
To come down from this tree.** (*Wave arm, motioning to come down.*)

**Here's what Jesus has to say,
Has to say, has to say.** (*Whisper.*)
**Here's what Jesus has to say
"I'll come to your house today."** (*Put fingertips together to make rooftop.*)

**Zacchaeus gave back what he took,
What he took, what he took.** (*Pretend to give.*)
**Zacchaeus gave back what he took.
He's no longer a crook!** (*Wipe hands clean.*)

Remembering God's Word

Each four- or five-week module focuses on a key Bible verse. The key verse for this module is "Never become tired of doing good" (2 Thessalonians 3:13).

This module's key verse will remind children to do what's right. Have fun using these ideas any time during the lessons on Zacchaeus.

All Tuckered Out

Have children spread out. Call out the following instructions.

- **Jump up and down.**
- **Hop on one foot.**
- **Do jumping jacks.**
- **Wiggle your arms and legs.**
- **Reach for the floor, then the ceiling.**
- **March around the room.**

When you've read all the instructions, have everyone sit down. Ask:

- **How do you feel?** (Hot; tired; out of breath.)
- **What made you feel that way?** (Jumping, following your directions.)

Say: **Second Thessalonians 3:13 says "Never become tired of doing good." Our game sure made us tired! But God doesn't want us to get tired of doing good things. Let's lay down and rest while we say the verse one more time.**

Lead children in saying the verse as they rest.

Stand Up, Sit Down

Lead children in singing "Never Tire," to the tune of "Frère Jacques." Form two groups. Have groups take turns springing up, singing a line, and crouching down.

Sing

Never tire	**Second Thessalonians**
Never tire	**Second Thessalonians**
Of doing good	**Three thirteen**
Of doing good,	**Three thirteen.**

After you sing the song, have children repeat the key verse together.

Story Enhancements

Make Bible stories come alive in your classroom by setting out sensory items, or creating wall displays or bulletin board ideas. The following ideas will get you started.

Come to Our House

Have children work together to prepare a simple snack such as crackers and cheese. After children have set out their snack, invite parents to join you. Have children tell their parents about Jesus coming to Zacchaeus' house.

Tree Ornaments

Have children help you create a Zacchaeus bulletin board. Twist paper grocery sacks into a tree shape and staple it to a bulletin board. Photocopy the Jesus and Zacchaeus figures (p. 148). Staple the Zacchaeus figure in the tree. Staple the Jesus figure on the ground below the tree.

Each week, set out tape, scissors, and green construction paper squares. Help children fold the paper in half and cut or tear half of a heart shape. Have children share good things they've done then tape the leaves to the tree. Encourage children to cover Zacchaeus with heart leaves.

Jesus & Zacchaeus

Permission to photocopy this handout from Group's Hands-On Bible Curriculum™ for Preschool granted for local church use.
Copyright © Group Publishing, Inc., Box 481, Loveland, CO 80539.

Seeing Is Believing

> **The Point**
>
> ✏️ Jesus wants us to love him.

The Bible Basis

Luke 19:1-4. Zacchaeus learns to love Jesus.

Zacchaeus served the hated Roman government as a tax collector. He accumulated great wealth by charging more than the fair amount and keeping the "profits" for himself. The people of Jericho despised Zacchaeus as a thief and a swindler. But when Jesus came through Jericho, Zacchaeus joined the crowd that pressed closer to see the miracle worker. Everyone had heard of Jesus' teaching and miracles. Unfortunately, Zacchaeus' diminutive size made it impossible for him to see Jesus over the crowd. And no one would budge to allow a crooked tax collector a closer view! So Zacchaeus climbed a sycamore tree to see the famous prophet from Nazareth.

Three- and 4-year-olds know what it's like to be too little to do something important. They know the disappointment that comes when they're too small to reach a toy on a high shelf, go on a ride at an amusement park, or see over the crowd at a parade. Like the crowd in Jericho, adults may be so caught up in their own interests that they fail to see preschoolers' frustrations. Preschoolers need to have opportunities to feel "big" and important. Use this lesson to help your students learn that no matter how small they are Jesus loves them, and they can learn to love Jesus, too.

Getting The Point

✏️ **Jesus wants us to love him.**

It's important to say The Point just as it's written in each activity. Repeating The Point over and over will help children remember it and apply it to their lives.

Children will
- experience being too short to see over a crowd,
- hear a story about Zacchaeus trying to see Jesus,
- learn that Jesus loves them just as they are, and
- think of ways they can show their love for Jesus.

✏️ **The Point**

This Lesson at a Glance

Before the lesson, collect the necessary items for the activities you plan to use. Refer to the Classroom Supplies and Learning Lab Supplies columns to determine what you'll need. Remember to make photocopies of the "Today I Learned..." handout (p. 158) to send home with your children.

Section	Minutes	What Children Will Do	Classroom Supplies	Learning Lab Supplies
Welcome Time	up to 5	**Welcome!**—Receive name tags and be greeted by the teacher.	"Angel Name Tags" handouts (p. 30)	
Let's Get Started Direct children to one or more of the Let's Get Started activities until everyone arrives.	up to 12	**Option 1: Option 1: Tall Towers**—Build tall block towers to measure their height.	Blocks	
	up to 12	**Option 2: Coin Prints**—Lay foil over coins and make rubbings.	Tape, pennies, nickels, dimes, quarters, aluminum foil	
	up to 12	**Option 3: Tree Treats**—Fill celery "trees" with peanut butter and raisins.	Raisins, peanut butter, plastic knives, celery, plate	
Pick-Up Song	up to 5	**Now It's Time**—Sing a song as they pick up toys and gather for Bible-Story Time.	Cassette player	Cassette: "Now It's Time"
Bible-Story Time	up to 8	**Setting the Stage**—Try to see a picture of Jesus through a crowd of children.	"Jesus and Zacchaeus " handout (p. 148)	
	up to 5	**Bible Song and Prayer Time**—Sing a song, bring out the Bible, and pray together.	Bible, cassette player	Tree stamp and ink pad, cassette: "We Are Glad..."
	up to 8	**Hear the Bible Story**—Hear the story of Zacchaeus from Luke 19:1-8, then sing a song.	Bible, cassette player	Bible Big Book: Zacchaeus, cassette: "Zacchaeus," "Did You Ever See Zacchaeus?"
	up to 5	**Do the Bible Story**—Collect hearts and toss them up in the air as they sing a song.	Construction paper, scissors, grocery sack	
Practicing The Point	up to 8	**I'm Rich!**—Teach Whiskers how to show his love for Jesus.	Whiskers the Mouse, bag of pennies	
Closing	up to 5	**Loving Jesus**—Learn a new way to tell Jesus they love him, then enjoy tree treats.	Tree treats from Option 3	
For Extra Time		For extra-time ideas and supplies, see page 157.		

Jesus wants us to love him.

Welcome Time

Welcome! (up to 5 minutes)

- Bend down and make eye contact with children as they arrive.
- Greet each child individually with an enthusiastic smile.
- Thank each child for coming to class today.
- As children arrive, ask them about last week's "Today I Learned..." discussion. Use questions such as "What did you tell your family about the net full of fish?" and "Tell me about a time you trusted Jesus to help you this week."

Say: **Today we're going to learn that**  **Jesus wants us to love him.**

- Hand out the angel name tags children made during Lesson 1 and help them attach the name tags to their clothing. If some of the name tags were damaged or if children weren't in class that week, have them make new name tags using the photocopiable handout on page 30.
- Direct children to the Let's Get Started activities you've set up.

The Point

Let's Get Started

Set up one or more of the following activities for children to do as they arrive. After you greet each child, invite him or her to choose an activity.

Circulate among the children to offer help as needed and direct children's conversation toward the point of today's lesson. Ask questions such as "How do you feel when you're too small to do something?" or "How do you show that you love someone?"

OPTION 1: Tall Towers (up to 12 minutes)

Set out blocks and encourage children to build towers that are the same height as they are. As children build, point out that some towers are shorter and some are taller. Explain that today's Bible story is about a short man who learned to love Jesus. Remind children that ⬤ Jesus wants us to love him.

OPTION 2: Coin Prints (up to 12 minutes)

Before this activity, tape pennies, nickels, and quarters to a table. Be sure to put the tape only on the sides of the coins that are facing the table. Caution children not to remove the coins from the table or put them in their mouths!

Set out aluminum foil squares. Show children how to rub the foil over the coins with their thumbs until coin prints appear. Have them try rubbing each different coin. Tell children that today's Bible story is about a greedy man who stole other people's money.

OPTION 3: Tree Treats (up to 12 minutes)

Set out raisins, peanut butter, plastic knives, and celery stalks with leaves. Help children fill the celery trees with peanut butter, then add raisins to represent Zacchaeus' footprints.

Talk with children about times they've played in trees. Explain that today they'll hear about a man who climbed a tree to see Jesus. Make one stalk for every two students. Cut the stalks in half and set them aside until the Closing.

When everyone has arrived and you're ready to move on to Bible-Story Time, encourage the children to finish what they're doing and get ready to clean up.

Pick-Up Song

Now It's Time (up to 5 minutes)

Lead children in singing "Now It's Time" with the *cassette tape,* to the tune of "The Mulberry Bush." Encourage children to sing along as they help clean up the room.

Sing

Now it's time to clean up our room,
Clean up our room,
Clean up our room.
Now it's time to clean up our room
And put our things away.

Will you help me? Yes, I will.
Yes, I will.
Yes, I will!
Will you help me? Yes, I will.
I'll help you right away.

(Repeat)

Bible-Story Time

Setting the Stage (up to 8 minutes)

Before this activity, photocopy the "Jesus and Zacchaeus" handout (p. 148) and cut out the picture of Jesus.

Tell children you'll clap three times to get their attention. Explain that when you clap three times, the children are to stop what they're doing and repeat the clap. Practice this signal a few times. Encourage children to respond quickly so you'll have time for all the fun activities you've planned.

Have children gather in the story area. Ask:

● **What did you make or do when you came to our class today?** (Built a tall tower with blocks; rubbed coins and made a print; made tree snacks.)

Say: **Some of you built towers, some of you made coin prints, and some of you made tree treats. You were all learning important things about our Bible story. If you built a tower of blocks, stand up and pat the top of your head. Show us how big and tall you are!** (Pause) **If you made coin prints, stand up and rub your hands together.** (Pause) **If you made tree treats, stand up and stretch out your arms like a tree.** (Pause)

Say: **Let's all pretend we're trees and stand up as tall as we can. Now pretend we're swaying in the wind. Trees are very tall, so stand up on your tiptoes.**

Jesus wants us to love him.

Have children sit down. Say: **Our Bible story is about a short man named Zacchaeus who climbed up in a tall tree so he could see Jesus.**

Form two groups. Have one group stand shoulder to shoulder in a tight circle. Have the rest of the children stand behind the first group. Say: **I'm going to put this picture of Jesus in the middle of this crowd.** Hold the picture of Jesus at children's waist level. Encourage the outside children to try to see the picture through the "crowd." After a moment, provide low chairs and let children peer over the circle.

Say: **Look, look what can you see? Please find the picture of Jesus for me. If you can find it, clap—one, two, three!**

Have groups trade places and repeat the activity. Then say: **Now you know how Zacchaeus felt when he couldn't see Jesus.** 🖊 **Jesus wants us to love him. Let's find out how Zacchaeus learned to love Jesus.**

🔵 **The Point**

Bible Song and Prayer Time (up to 5 minutes)

Say: **Now it's time to choose a Bible person to bring me the Bible marked with today's Bible story. As we sing our Bible song, we'll pass around our special Bible. The person who's holding the Bible when the music stops will be our Bible person today.**

Lead children in singing "We Are Glad to Read the Bible" with the *cassette tape,* to the tune of "Did You Ever See a Lassie?" As you sing, pass around the special Bible.

Sing

**We are glad to read the Bible,
The Bible, the Bible.
We are glad to read the Bible
For it is God's Book.**

**We'll hear Bible stories
And learn about God's love.
We are glad to read the Bible
For it is God's Book.**

When the music stops, invite the child who's holding the Bible to bring it to you. Stamp the child's hand with the *tree stamp* and thank the child for bringing you the Bible. Then stamp the other children's hands. Return the *tree stamp and ink pad* to the Learning Lab.

Say: **I'm thankful for** (name of child who brought the Bible) **and I'm thankful for everyone in our class today. Let's thank God together for all our friends in this class.**

Lead children in singing "We Are Glad to Pray Together" with the *cassette tape,* to the tune of "Did You Ever See a Lassie?" If you want to include the names of all the children in your class, sing the song without the cassette and repeat the naming section. If you choose to use the cassette, vary the names you use each week.

Sing

**We are glad to pray together,
Together, together.
We are glad to pray together
And give thanks to God.**

Lead children in folding their
hands and bowing their heads as
you continue to sing.

Thank you for (name),
And (name), **and** (name).
**Thank you, God, for every person
Who's here in our class.**

(Repeat)

Jesus wants us to love him.

Hear the Bible Story (up to 8 minutes)

Have children gather around you. Open the Bible to Luke 19. Say: **Our Bible story comes from the book of Luke in the Bible.** Bring out the *Bible Big Book: Zacchaeus.* Say: **Our *Bible Big Book* shows us pictures of our Bible story. Let's listen to the story of Zacchaeus on our *cassette tape.***

Show children the *Big Book* pictures as you play the "Zacchaeus" segment of the cassette. Turn the pages when you hear the chime. After the story, ask:
● **Why was Zacchaeus up in the tree?** (He was short; he wanted to see Jesus; he wanted to learn to love Jesus.)
● **Why did Jesus go to Zacchaeus' house?** (To eat; to tell him to give the money away; to be his friend.)

Say: **Jesus loved Zacchaeus very much, and Jesus wanted Zacchaeus to love him. How did Zacchaeus show that he loved Jesus?** (When he gave the money away; when he said he was sorry; by being nice.)

Say: **It must have been hard for Zacchaeus to give back the money he took, but he wanted to show that he loved Jesus. How can you show that you love Jesus?** (Be his friend; tell him I love him; talk to him.)

◗ The Point

Say: **Zacchaeus learned to love Jesus. ◗ Jesus wants us to love him, just like Zacchaeus did. Let's stand up and learn a song that reminds us that Zacchaeus loved Jesus.**

Lead children in singing "Did You Ever See Zacchaeus?" with the *cassette tape,* to the tune of "Did You Ever See a Lassie?" The song is recorded twice.

Sing

Did you ever see Zacchaeus *(hand over eyes across brow),*
Zacchaeus, Zacchaeus?
Did you ever see Zacchaeus
Way up in a tree? *(Point up high.)*

He looked 'round for Jesus *(turn around in a circle),*
Then climbed up to see him. *(Do climbing motions.)*
Did you ever see Zacchaeus *(hand over eyes across brow)*
Way up in a tree? *(Point up high.)*

Jesus saw Zacchaeus *(hand over eyes across brow)*
Zacchaeus, Zacchaeus.
Jesus saw Zacchaeus
Way up in that tree. *(Point up high.)*

"Zacchaeus, come down now." *(Wave towards self.)*
"I'm coming to your house." *(Point at another person.)*
Jesus saw Zacchaeus *(hand over eyes across brow)*
Way up in that tree. *(Point up high.)*

Do the Bible Story (up to 5 minutes)

Before class, cut out three construction paper hearts for each child. Have children close their eyes while you scatter the paper hearts on the floor. Then have children open their eyes. Say: ◗ **Jesus wants us to love him. Let's play a game to help us remember to love Jesus. See how many hearts you can pick up while we sing a song.**

◗ The Point

Lead children in singing "Jesus Wants Us to Love Him" to the tune of "London Bridge." Have children pick up the hearts while they're singing the first three lines and then toss the hearts in the air when they sing, "I love Jesus!"

Jesus wants us to love him.

**Jesus wants us to love him,
To love him, to love him.**

**Jesus wants us to love him.
I LOVE JESUS!**

Repeat the song several times, then collect the hearts. Ask:

● **What does Jesus want us to do?** (Love him; be nice; come to church.)

Say: **That's right!** ✏ **Jesus wants us to love him. Jesus also wants us to tell others that we love him. We can tell someone right now—our friend Whiskers!**

● **The Point**

Practicing The Point

I'm Rich! (up to 8 minutes)

Before class, seal a handful of pennies in a plastic sandwich bag. Have Whiskers hold the bag between his paws as you present the following script. When you finish the script, put Whiskers away and out of sight.

I'm Rich!

PUPPET SCRIPT

Teacher: Whiskers, what do you have in your bag? It jingles when you shake it.

Whiskers: (Shaking the bag) I have lots of money.

Teacher: Wow! How much money do you have?

Whiskers: Hmm, I'm not sure. But I know it's a lot!

Teacher: Can we help you count it?

Whiskers: If you promise to be careful. I don't want to lose any.
(Have Whiskers pour the money out of the bag.)

Teacher: Children, can you help me count Whiskers' pennies?
(Count pennies slowly and deliberately.)

Whiskers: Wow! I have that much money! I must be rich!

Teacher: You are rich. Where did you get your money?

Whiskers: I've been finding it all over our house. There was some on top of my parents' dresser, some in my mom's purse, and my brother left some on the kitchen table.

Teacher: (Horrified) Whiskers, that's not your money. It belongs to other people in your family. We've been learning about a man who took other people's money. Children, can you tell Whiskers about Zacchaeus?
(Help children tell Whiskers how Zacchaeus took people's money, then gave it back to show how much he loved Jesus.)

Whiskers: Wow! I guess I was wrong to take this money. I

(Continued)

wonder what I should do now.

Teacher: Children, what do you think Whiskers should do with the money he took?

(Help children think of things such as returning the money, asking for forgiveness, or putting the money back where he found it.)

Whiskers: I guess if I gave the money back, it would show that I'm sorry.

Teacher: Right! Today we learned that  Jesus wants us to love him. Zacchaeus wanted to show that he loved Jesus more than he loved the money he'd collected.

Whiskers: Well, I want to show that I love Jesus. I'd better give back these pennies right now. Thanks for helping me

◖ The Point

TODAY I LEARNED . . .

We believe Christian education extends beyond the classroom into the home. Photocopy the "Today I Learned..." handout (p. 158) for this week and send it home with your children. Encourage parents to use the handout to plan meaningful family activities to reinforce this week's topic. Follow up the "Today I Learned..." activities next week by asking children what their families did.

Closing

Loving Jesus (up to 5 minutes)

◖ The Point

Say: ◖ **Jesus wants us to love him. We can show our love for Jesus in lots of different ways. Let's use sign language to show we love Jesus.**

Teach children these simple, signs to express their love for Jesus.

I: Press your hand to your chest and hold up your little finger.

Love: Cross your hands across your chest.

Jesus: Touch your right palm with your left middle finger and then your left palm with your right middle finger.

Have children say and sign, "I love Jesus" several times. Then pray: **Dear God, thank you for your Son, Jesus, who loves us so much. Help us show how much we love Jesus. Amen.**

◖ The Point

Give each child a half of a tree treat from Option 3 and say: ◖ **Jesus wants us to love him. As you eat your tree treat, remember how Zacchaeus learned to love Jesus.**

Jesus wants us to love him.

For Extra Time

If you have a long class time or want to add additional elements to your lesson, try one of the following activities.

LIVELY LEARNING: Coin Capers

Have children sit in a circle and cup their hands behind their backs, facing up. Give children each a coin to hold in their cupped hands. Have one child pretend to be Zacchaeus and go around the circle touching each person's coin. When "Zacchaeus" is ready, he or she can take a coin instead of just touching it. The student whose coin was taken will jump up and chase Zacchaeus around the circle. If Zacchaeus reaches the other child's place without being tagged, the child whose coin was taken becomes the new Zacchaeus. If the child tags Zacchaeus, Zacchaeus must give the coin back and sit in the middle of the circle. Keep playing until everyone has a chance to be Zacchaeus. As children play, remind them that Zacchaeus took other people's money and then gave it back to show that he loved Jesus.

MAKE TO TAKE: Love Baskets

Distribute 8×10-inch paper hearts in a variety of colors. Each child will need two hearts. Use a hole punch to make five holes around each heart, two on each side and one on the bottom. For each child, set out a 2-foot length of yarn with one end taped. Show children how to weave the yarn "needles" through the holes to make heart baskets. As children work, tell them that ✎ Jesus wants us to love him.

● **The Point**

TREAT TO EAT: Heart Treats

Have children use heart-shaped cookie cutters to cut pieces of bread. Set out peanut butter and jam and help children make heart-shaped sandwiches. Before children eat, have them remind each other that ✎ Jesus wants us to love him.

● **The Point**

STORY PICTURE: Zacchaeus Wants to See Jesus

Give each child a photocopy of the "Today I Learned..." handout (p. 158). Have children color their handouts with crayons. Set out glue sticks and green tissue paper. Let children rub their tree pictures with a glue stick then tear off small tissue paper "leaves" to stick on the tree. As children work, remind them that ✎ Jesus wants us to love him.

● **The Point**

TODAY I LEARNED . . .

The Point ✏ Jesus wants us to love him.

Today your child learned that Jesus wants us to love him. Children heard a Bible story about Zacchaeus and how he learned to love Jesus. They talked about ways they can show their love for Jesus.

Verse to Learn

"Never become tired of doing good" (2 Thessalonians 3:13).

Ask Me . . .

● How did Zacchaeus show his love for Jesus?

● Why is it important to show Jesus that you love him?

● If our family loves Jesus, how should we treat others?

Family Fun

● Find a large tree in your yard or in a nearby park. Lie under the tree and look up into its branches. Imagine looking up and seeing Zacchaeus in the tree! Hold hands and tell Jesus how much you love him.

Zacchaeus Wants to See Jesus (Luke 19:1-4)

Permission to photocopy this handout from Group's Hands-On Bible Curriculum™ for Preschool granted for local church use. Copyright © Group Publishing, Inc., Box 481, Loveland, CO 80539.

LESSON 10

A Kind Invitation

The Point

🖊 Jesus wants us to be kind.

The Bible Basis

Luke 19:5-7. Jesus calls Zacchaeus down from the tree.

As a fraudulent tax collector, Zacchaeus wasn't used to warm greetings. The people of Jericho probably went out of their way to avoid him. Yet Jesus went out of his way to show kindness and acceptance to Zacchaeus. The towns-people felt surprise, even outrage, that Jesus would invite himself to the home of such a sinner. But Jesus' kindness changed Zacchaeus' heart, causing Zacchaeus to return all he'd taken—and more!

The 3- and 4-year-olds in your class enjoy being kind. They love to give hugs, hold hands, and help around the house. But they also experience unkindness when others play roughly, don't share, leave playmates out of a game, or call people mean names. You can teach your preschoolers that kind-ness helps people feel better and can even change hearts. In this lesson, chil-dren will discover the power of kindness and understand why Jesus wants them to be kind.

Getting The Point

🖊 **Jesus wants us to be kind.**

It's important to say The Point just as it's written in each activity. Re-peating The Point over and over will help the children remember it and apply it to their lives.

Children will
● learn that Jesus was kind to Zacchaeus,
● practice being kind,
● show kindness to Whiskers, and
● sing a song about kindness.

🖊 **The Point**

Jesus wants us to be kind.

This Lesson at a Glance

Before the lesson, collect the necessary items for the activities you plan to use. Refer to the Classroom Supplies and Learning Lab Supplies columns to determine what you'll need. Remember to make photocopies of the "Today I Learned..." handout (p. 168) to send home with your children.

Section	Minutes	What Children Will Do	Classroom Supplies	Learning Lab Supplies
Welcome Time	up to 5	**Welcome!**—Receive name tags and be greeted by the teacher.	"Angel Name Tags" handouts (p. 30)	
Let's Get Started Direct children to one or more of the Let's Get Started activities until everyone arrives.	up to 12	**Option 1: Praise Parade**—March in a procession like the one Jesus may have been in as he went through Jericho.	Dolls, stuffed animals, crepe paper, dress-up clothes	
	up to 12	**Option 2: Kindness Cutouts**—Prepare a snack that will show kindness to Whiskers.	Cheese slices, cookie cutters, paper plates	
	up to 12	**Option 3: Coin Collectors**—Make coins from aluminum foil.	Aluminum-foil squares	
Pick-Up Song	up to 5	**Now It's Time**—Sing a song as they pick up toys and gather for Bible-Story Time.	Cassette player	Cassette: "Now It's Time"
Bible-Story Time	up to 8	**Setting the Stage**—Play a game to express kindness to each other.	Colored paper, scissors	
	up to 5	**Bible Song and Prayer Time**—Sing a song, bring out the Bible, and pray together.	Bible, cassette player	Tree stamp and ink pad, cassette: "We Are Glad..."
	up to 10	**Hear the Bible Story**—Act out the story of Zacchaeus from Luke 19:1-10.	Bible, foil coins from Option 3	
	up to 5	**Do the Bible Story**—Sing "I'm Coming to Your House" and act out ways to show kindness.		
Practicing The Point	up to 5	**Mouse Munchies**—Hear how Whiskers' family treated him kindly and then share a snack.	Whiskers the Mouse, napkins, crackers, cheese cutouts from Option 2	
Closing	up to 5	**Kind and Loving Chorus**—Sing a song and then pray, asking God to help them be kind this week.	Cassette player	Cassette: "Be Kind and Loving"
For Extra Time		For extra-time ideas and supplies, see page 167.		

Jesus wants us to be kind.

Welcome Time

Welcome! (up to 5 minutes)

- Bend down and make eye contact with children as they arrive.
- Greet each child individually with an enthusiastic smile.
- Thank each child for coming to class today.
- As children arrive, ask them about last week's "Today I Learned..." discussion. Use questions such as "What did you tell your family about Jesus and Zacchaeus? and "How did your family show that you love Jesus?"
- Say: **Today we're going to learn that ● Jesus wants us to be kind.**
- Hand out the angel name tags children made during Lesson 1 and help them attach the name tags to their clothing. If some of the name tags were damaged or if children weren't in class that week, have them make new name tags using the photocopiable handout on page 30.
- Direct children to the Let's Get Started activities you've set up.

● The Point

Let's Get Started

Set up one or more of the following activities for children to do as they arrive. After you greet each child, invite him or her to choose an activity.

Circulate among the children to offer help as needed and direct children's conversation toward the point of today's lesson. Ask questions such as "What's it like to visit with someone you think is special?" or "How does it feel when someone is kind to you?

☐ OPTION 1: Praise Parade (up to 12 minutes)

Set out dolls, stuffed animals, crepe paper streamers, and dress-up clothes. You also might want to play a cassette of marching music. Tell children you're going to have a parade. Create a "street" with two rows of chairs. Encourage children to line the street with the dolls and animals and then parade down the center as they wave their streamers. They can pretend that they're Jesus and his followers walking into Jericho.

☐ OPTION 2: Kindness Cutouts (up to 12 minutes)

Set out cheese slices, cookie cutters, and paper plates. Help children use the cookie cutters to cut cheese slices into interesting shapes. Place the cheese cutouts on a tray and cover the tray with plastic wrap to keep the cheese from drying out. Children will put the cheese on crackers later in the lesson.

Remind children that Jesus went to Zacchaeus' house for a meal. Tell children that ● Jesus wants us to be kind, just as he was kind to Zacchaeus. Explain that Whiskers might enjoy this snack a little later.

● The Point

☐ Option 3: Coin Collectors (up to 12 minutes)

Set out several 4-inch aluminum foil squares. Have children mold the foil into small, flat circles to form pretend coins. Be sure children don't put the "coins" in their mouths. Remind children that Zacchaeus took money from lots of people, but then he gave all of it back—and more!

If children finish early, have them make extra coins to share. Later in the lesson, you'll need two coins for each child in your class.

When everyone has arrived and you're ready to move on to Bible-Story Time, encourage the children to finish what they're doing and get ready to clean up.

Pick-Up Song

Now It's Time (up to 5 minutes)

Lead children in singing "Now It's Time" with the *cassette tape,* to the tune of "The Mulberry Bush." Encourage children to sing along as they help clean up the room. Today while you're cleaning up, ask an adult helper to secretly and quietly set Whiskers somewhere up high in the classroom.

Sing

Now it's time to clean up our room,
Clean up our room,
Clean up our room.
Now it's time to clean up our room
And put our things away.

Will you help me? Yes, I will.
Yes, I will.
Yes, I will!
Will you help me? Yes, I will.
I'll help you right away.

(Repeat)

Bible-Story Time

Setting the Stage (up to 8 minutes)

Before class, cut pairs of paper hearts. Make each pair different.

Tell children that you'll clap three times to get their attention. Explain that when you clap three times, the children are to stop what they're doing and repeat the clap. Practice this signal a few times. Encourage children to respond quickly so you'll have time for all the fun activities you've planned.

Ask:

● **What did you make or do when you came to class today?** (Cut cheese slices; had a parade; made coins.)

Say: **Some of you had a lively parade, some of you made a snack for us to enjoy later, and some of you made coins. You were all learning important things about our Bible story. We're going to learn that**

🖊 Jesus wants us to be kind. Since Valentine's Day is almost here, let's play a valentine game to help us show love and kindness to each other.

Hand each child a paper heart. Say: **When I say "go," walk around the room, shake hands with everyone you meet, and say, "If you have the heart that matches mine, I will be your valentine." When you find the person whose heart matches yours, hug each other, trade hearts, and sit down together.**

When everyone is seated, collect the hearts. Ask:

● **What was it like to give handshakes and hugs?** (Fun; nice; it made me happy.)

Say: **It's fun to be kind and loving.** 🖊 **Jesus wants us to be kind. Today we'll hear how Jesus and Zacchaeus were kind. We'll learn how we can be kind, too!**

Bible Song and Prayer Time (up to 5 minutes)

Say: **Now it's time to choose a Bible person to bring me the Bible marked with today's Bible story. As we sing our Bible song, we'll pass around our special Bible. The person who's holding the Bible when the music stops will be our Bible person today.**

Lead children in singing "We Are Glad to Read the Bible" with the *cassette tape,* to the tune of "Did You Ever See a Lassie?" As you sing, pass around the special Bible.

Sing 🎵

We are glad to read the Bible,
The Bible, the Bible.
We are glad to read the Bible
For it is God's Book.

We'll hear Bible stories
And learn about God's love.
We are glad to read the Bible
For it is God's Book.

When the music stops, invite the child who's holding the Bible to bring it to you. Stamp the child's hand with the *tree stamp* and thank the child for bringing you the Bible. Then stamp the other children's hands. Return the *tree stamp and ink pad* to the Learning Lab.

Say: **I'm thankful for** (name of child who brought the Bible) **and I'm thankful for everyone in our class today. Let's thank God together for all our friends in this class.**

Lead children in singing "We Are Glad to Pray Together" with the *cassette tape,* to the tune of "Did You Ever See a Lassie?" If you want to include the names of all the children in your class, sing the song without the cassette and repeat the naming section. If you choose to use the cassette, vary the names you use each week.

Sing 🎵

We are glad to pray together,
Together, together.
We are glad to pray together
And give thanks to God.

Lead children in folding their
hands and bowing their heads as
you continue to sing.

Thank you for (name),
And (name), and (name).
Thank you, God, for every person
Who's here in our class.

(Repeat)

Jesus wants us to be kind.

Hear the Bible Story (up to 10 minutes)

Have children gather around you. Open the Bible to Luke 19. Say: **Our Bible story comes from the book of Luke in the Bible. We read this story from our *Bible Big Book* last week. Let's act it out this time. I need four volunteers—one to be Jesus, one to be Zacchaeus, and two children to be the tree.** Choose four willing, outgoing volunteers. Have the tree volunteers stand on either side of a chair with their arms outstretched like tree branches. **The rest of you will be people in the town. I'll give you each two foil coins to use as you act out the story.** Distribute the coins.

Read the following story slowly and encourage children to act out their parts.

Zacchaeus was a tax man *(Zacchaeus bows)*
Who took lots of money.
When he took too much from people *(Zacchaeus collects coins)*,
They didn't think it was funny! *(People frown.)*

So no one liked Zacchaeus. *(People turn away from Zacchaeus.)*
He didn't have a friend!
But he kept on taking money *(Zacchaeus collects more coins)*,
For he loved to buy and spend! *(Zacchaeus holds up the money.)*

One day Jesus passed through town *(people make path for Jesus)*,
And everyone wanted to see! *(People follow Jesus.)*
The crowd was tall. Zacchaeus was small *(Zacchaeus tries to see around everyone)*,
So Zacchaeus climbed a tree. *(Zacchaeus climbs on "tree" chair.)*

But Jesus called Zacchaeus down *(Jesus beckons to Zacchaeus)*
And went to his house to stay. *(Zacchaeus and Jesus walk away.)*
For Jesus loved Zacchaeus *(Jesus hugs Zacchaeus)*—
He loves us all that way!

Because of Jesus' kindness,
Zacchaeus changed that day!
He asked forgiveness for his sins *(Zacchaeus kneels)*
And gave half his possessions away! *(Zacchaeus returns the coins.)*

Have children change roles, then repeat the poem once or twice. Collect the coins and gather children in a circle. Ask:

● **Why was Jesus kind to Zacchaeus?** (Because he loved him; Jesus loves everyone; Jesus wanted him to change.)

● **What kind thing did Zacchaeus do?** (He gave back the money he'd taken.)

● **Why do you think Jesus wants us to be kind?** (Because it makes people feel good; because it's better than being mean.)

✎ The Point

Say: **Because Jesus was kind, Zacchaeus learned to be kind, too.** ✎ **Jesus wants us to be kind so others will learn from us. There are lots of ways to be kind to others! We'll get to practice one way in just a little while. But first, let's play a game to remind us that Jesus was kind to Zacchaeus.**

Do the Bible Story (up to 5 minutes)

Form a circle. Ask one child to pretend to be Jesus and to stand in the center. Have the rest of the group hold hands and walk around in a circle as they sing "I'm Coming to Your House," to the tune of "The Farmer's in the Dell."

Sing

"I'm coming to your house,
"I'm coming to your house."

Jesus told Zacchaeus,
"I'm coming to your house."

Direct "Jesus" to select someone to be "Zacchaeus" and have that child come to the center. Help the children in the center act out one way to show kindness, such as giving a hug. Then send both children back to the circle and choose a new Jesus.

Repeat the game until everyone has had a turn to be Jesus or Zacchaeus. Say: **When Jesus went to Zacchaeus' house, Zacchaeus learned to be kind.** 🖊 **Jesus wants us to be kind, too. Let's practice showing kindness to our friend Whiskers by sharing our snack with him. First, help me call him. Whiskers! Whiskers!**

🖊 **The Point**

Practicing The Point

Mouse Munchies (up to 5 minutes)

Bring out Whiskers the Mouse and go through the following puppet script. When you finish the script, take Whiskers with you to your snack area.

Mouse Munchies

PUPPET SCRIPT

Whiskers: Hi, everyone! What's going on today?

Teacher: Well, Whiskers, we've been learning about how Jesus showed kindness to Zacchaeus, even when Zacchaeus had done bad things. Children, why don't you tell Whiskers what Jesus did when he met Zacchaeus?

(Help children tell how Jesus went to Zacchaeus' house and helped Zacchaeus learn about being kind.)

Whiskers: Wow! Something like that happened to me this week!

Teacher: Someone was kind to you? Who?

Whiskers: My family! Remember how I took some of their money? Well, when I gave the money back, they didn't get mad at me! In fact, my dad hugged me and told me he was proud that I'd returned the money! They all forgave me and said they loved me, even though I'd done something wrong!

Teacher: They were kind to you! Well, we've come to be kind,

(Continued)

Jesus wants us to be kind.

too. The children would like to share their snack with you!

Whiskers: With me? But why?

Teacher: Because  Jesus wants us to be kind.

Whiskers: Oooh, I like it when people are kind to me. It makes me want to be kind right back!

Teacher: Are you ready for your snack?

Whiskers: You bet! *(Pausing)* Is it something with cheese?

Teacher: It sure is!

Whiskers: Yippee!

Bring out the cheese cutouts from Option 2. Give each child a napkin, two cheese cutouts, and a few crackers. You may pretend to feed Whiskers while children enjoy their snack.

TODAY I LEARNED...

We believe Christian education extends beyond the classroom into the home. Photocopy the "Today I Learned..." handout (p. 168) for this week and send it home with your children. Encourage parents to use the handout to plan meaningful family activities to reinforce this week's topic. Follow up the "Today I Learned..." activities next week by asking children what their families did.

Closing

Kind and Loving Chorus (up to 5 minutes)

Say: **It was nice to see you all being so kind to Whiskers! I think he really enjoyed it! The book of Ephesians in the Bible tells us to "be kind and loving to each other." Let's sing a song to help us remember that.**

Form pairs and have partners face each other. Show children how to clap their hands and then pat their partners' hands as you lead them in singing "Be Kind and Loving" with the *cassette tape,* to the tune of "Ten Little Indians." After each verse, pause the tape and have children find new partners.

Sing

Be kind and loving to each other.   Be kind and loving to each other.
Be kind and loving to each other.   Ephesians 4:32.

(Repeat twice)

The Point

Say:  **Jesus wants us to be kind, just like he was kind to Zacchaeus. Let's pray for God to help us.** Pray: **Dear God, thank you for sending Jesus to show us what it means to be kind. Help us to be kind and loving to others this week. In Jesus' name, amen.**

For Extra Time

If you have a long class time or want to add additional elements to your lesson, try one of the following activities.

LIVELY LEARNING: Hurry to the House

Before this activity, build a simple block house at one end of the room. Place foil "coins" in a paper lunch sack and set it next to the house. Place an empty paper lunch sack at the opposite end of the room.

Form pairs and have them line up by the empty sack. Tell children that when Jesus went to Zacchaeus' house, Zacchaeus learned how to be kind; then Zacchaeus gave back the money he'd taken. Have pairs line up and hold hands or link arms. Have them take giant steps to the block house, take a coin, take giant steps back, and drop the coin in the sack. Continue until all the money is in the sack.

MAKE TO TAKE: Kindness Necklace

Cut out six small construction paper hearts for each child and punch a hole near the top of each heart. Set out bowls of rigatoni pasta or 1-inch lengths of drinking straws. Cut an 18-inch length of yarn for each child. Wrap one end with tape to use as a "needle" and tie a large knot in the other end. Demonstrate how to thread the paper hearts between the pieces of pasta. Encourage the children to wear their necklaces to remind them that ✏ Jesus wants us to be kind.

TREAT TO EAT: Table for Two

Set out graham crackers, mini-marshmallows, plastic knives, and a bowl of frosting or marshmallow creme. Have each child spread frosting on a graham cracker and then place it on four mini-marshmallows to make a table. Before children enjoy their snack, point out that Jesus and Zacchaeus shared a special meal together. Remind children that Jesus helped Zacchaeus learn to be kind.

STORY PICTURE: Jesus Goes to Zacchaeus' House

Give each child a photocopy of the "Today I Learned..." handout (p. 168). Let children cut or tear construction paper into small scraps. Set out glue sticks and show children how to glue the paper to Zacchaeus' house, mosaic-style. Allow them to color in the rest of the picture. Tell children that Jesus showed kindness to Zacchaeus, and ✏ Jesus wants us to be kind, too.

✏ **The Point**

TODAY I LEARNED . . .

The Point ✏ Jesus wants us to be kind.

Today your child learned that Jesus wants us to be kind. Children discovered that when Jesus was kind to Zacchaeus, Zacchaeus changed from a mean person to a nice person. They practiced showing kindness to others.

Verse to Learn

"Never become tired of doing good" (2 Thessalonians 3:13).

Ask Me . . .

● How do you think Zacchaeus felt when Jesus wanted to come home with him?

● Tell about a time someone was kind to you? How did you feel?

● Who can our family be kind to?

Family Fun

● Go on a Kindness Hunt this week. When you catch family members being kind, return the kindness by giving them a hug.

● During a meal this week, encourage family members to show kindness by serving, affirming, and helping each other.

Jesus Goes to Zacchaeus' House (Luke 19:5-7)

Permission to photocopy this handout from Group's Hands-On Bible Curriculum™ for Preschool granted for local church use. Copyright © Group Publishing, Inc., Box 481, Loveland, CO 80539.

LESSON 11

Sincerely Sorry

The Bible Basis

Luke 19:8. Zacchaeus shows that he is sorry.

We don't know what words passed between Zacchaeus and Jesus when they were together. But Jesus' love and kindness had a tremendous effect on Zacchaeus. Zacchaeus turned from his deceitful ways and responded to Jesus with a repentant heart. He pledged to give half of his possessions to the poor, then offered to return four times what he'd taken from people. Zacchaeus' words and actions demonstrated true repentance.

Preschoolers know when they've done something wrong, but they don't always know how to set things right. When children disobey or hurt others, parents or teachers may tell them to say they're sorry. But children need to realize that "sorry" is more than words—it includes showing genuine regret and determination to go in a new and better direction. This lesson will help children see that Zacchaeus' actions showed that he was sorry. They'll learn how they can apologize with more than words.

Getting The Point

✏ **Jesus wants us to be sorry when we do wrong.**

It's important to say The Point just as it's written in each activity. Repeating The Point over and over will help the children remember it and apply it to their lives.

Children will
● make Zacchaeus finger puppets,
● hear how Zacchaeus showed he was sorry,
● learn to show they're sorry, and
● teach Whiskers to say, "I'm sorry."

● **The Point**

This Lesson at a Glance

Before the lesson, collect the necessary items for the activities you plan to use. Refer to the Classroom Supplies and Learning Lab Supplies columns to determine what you'll need. Remember to make photocopies of the "Today I Learned..." handout (p. 180) to send home with your children.

Section	Minutes	What Children Will Do	Classroom Supplies	Learning Lab Supplies
Welcome Time	up to 5	**Welcome!**—Receive name tags and be greeted by the teacher.	"Angel Name Tags" handouts (p. 30)	
Let's Get Started Direct children to one or more of the Let's Get Started activities until everyone arrives.	up to 10	**Option 1: Finger-Puppet Fun**—Make Zacchaeus finger puppets.	"Zacchaeus Finger Puppet" handouts (p. 179), crayons, pencils, scissors	
	up to 10	**Option 2: Dough-See-Dough**—Hide and search for milk-carton caps in modeling dough.	Modeling dough, milk-carton caps	
	up to 10	**Option 3: Clean Hearts**—Make hearts that are clean on one side and dark on the other.	Dark-blue construction paper, soap flakes, water, clothespins, cotton balls	
Pick-Up Song	up to 5	**Now It's Time**—Sing a song as they pick up toys and gather for Bible-Story Time.	Cassette player	Cassette: "Now It's Time"
Bible-Story Time	up to 8	**Setting the Stage**—Respond to situations where they would need to say, "I'm sorry."	Paper hearts from Option 3	
	up to 5	**Bible Song and Prayer Time**—Sing a song, bring out the Bible, and pray together.	Bible, cassette player	Tree stamp and ink pad, cassette: "We Are Glad..."
	up to 8	**Hear the Bible Story**—Use their finger puppets as they hear the story of Zacchaeus from Luke 19:1-10.	Bible, cassette player, finger puppets from Option 1	*Bible Big Book:* Zacchaeus cassette: "Zacchaeus"
	up to 5	**Do the Bible Story**—Sing a song to remember what Zacchaeus did to show he was sorry.	Cassette player	Cassette: "Did You Ever See Zacchaeus?"
Practicing The Point	up to 8	**Sorry, Joey**—Teach Whiskers to say, "I'm sorry."	Whiskers the Mouse, toy truck	
Closing	up to 5	**A Show of Hands**—Use a finger play to tell the story of Zacchaeus, then pray together.		
For Extra Time		For extra-time ideas and supplies, see page 178.		

Jesus wants us to be sorry when we do wrong.

Welcome Time

Welcome! (up to 5 minutes)

- Bend down and make eye contact with children as they arrive.
- Greet each child individually with an enthusiastic smile.
- Thank each child for coming to class today.
- As children arrive, ask them about last week's "Today I Learned..." discussion. Use questions such as "How were you kind to others?" and "What kind things did your family do?"
- Say: **Today we're going to learn that** **Jesus wants us to be sorry.**
- Hand out the angel name tags children made during Lesson 1 and help them attach the name tags to their clothing. If some of the name tags were damaged or if children weren't in class that week, have them make new name tags using the photocopiable handout on page 30.
- Direct children to the Let's Get Started activities you've set up.

◉ The Point

Let's Get Started

Set up one or more of the following activities for children to do as they arrive. After you greet each child, invite him or her to choose an activity.

Circulate among the children to offer help as needed and direct children's conversation toward the point of today's lesson. Ask questions such as "What do you do when you hurt someone's feelings?" or "When is it good to say you're sorry?"

Option 1: Finger-Puppet Fun (up to 10 minutes)

Make a photocopy of the "Zacchaeus Finger Puppet" handout (p. 179) for each child. Cut out the puppets and use a hole punch to make holes where children's fingers will go. Let each child color a puppet and poke a pencil or crayon through the hole to make it big enough to fit comfortably on a finger. Have willing helpers make extra finger puppets for children who don't choose this option. As children are working, tell them that today they'll hear what Zacchaeus did to show that he was sorry.

Collect the finger puppets for use in "Hear the Bible Story."

> ✔ To make the puppets sturdier, you may want to glue them to a backing cut from a file folder or cereal box.

Option 2: Dough-See-Dough (up to 10 minutes)

Set out modeling dough and milk-carton caps. Form pairs and have each partner hide a few caps in a lump of dough. Instruct partners to trade dough with each other and see if they can find the caps. Explain that sometimes

The Point

when we do wrong things we can't see them, but we can feel them inside—just like the caps are inside the dough. Remind children that 🔵 Jesus wants us to be sorry when we do something wrong. Point out that when we say we're sorry, we feel better inside.

☐ Option 3: Clean Hearts (up to 10 minutes)

Before class, mix 1 cup of soap flakes, such as Ivory Snow, with 1/3 cup of water. Cut 8-inch hearts out of dark-blue construction paper, then clip clothespins to cotton balls to make paint daubers. Have children dab the soap mixture on one side of the paper hearts. Explain that the bad things Zacchaeus did made his heart dark and unhappy. But when he showed that he was sorry, Jesus made his heart clean and happy like the soapy side of the heart.

> ✔ You'll need one paper heart for each child in your class, so have volunteers make extras for children who don't choose this option.

When everyone has arrived and you're ready to move on to Bible-Story Time, encourage the children to finish what they're doing and get ready to clean up.

Pick-Up Song

Now It's Time (up to 5 minutes)

Lead children in singing "Now It's Time" with the *cassette tape*, to the tune of "The Mulberry Bush." Encourage children to sing along as they help clean up the room.

Sing

Now it's time to clean up our room,
Clean up our room,
Clean up our room.
Now it's time to clean up our room
And put our things away.

Will you help me? Yes, I will.
Yes, I will.
Yes, I will!
Will you help me? Yes, I will.
I'll help you right away.

(Repeat)

Jesus wants us to be sorry when we do wrong.

Bible-Story Time

Setting the Stage (up to 8 minutes)

Tell children that you'll clap three times to get their attention. Explain that when you clap three times, the children are to stop what they're doing and repeat the clap. Practice this signal a few times. Encourage children to respond quickly so you'll have time for all the fun activities you've planned.

Ask:

● **What did you make or do when you came to class today?** (Hid caps in modeling dough; put soap on paper hearts; made finger puppets.)

Say: **Some of you made finger puppets, some of you hid milk-carton caps in modeling dough, and some of you put soap on paper hearts. You were all doing important things to teach us about being sorry when we do things that are wrong.**

When you hid the milk-carton caps inside the dough, that was like hiding bad things in our hearts. When you painted the hearts with the soap, you learned that when we tell Jesus we're sorry, Jesus makes our hearts clean again. When you made finger puppets, you were getting ready to hear the story of Zacchaeus being sorry for taking money.

Let's play a game to think about times when we should say we're sorry.

Have children gather at one end of the room. Place the paper hearts from Option 3 on the other side of the room, with the dark sides facing up. Say: **I'll ask a question about a time when you might need to say you're sorry. If you should say sorry, jump up and say, "Sorry, Charlie!" Then hop to a paper heart, turn it over to the soapy side, then hop back. If you wouldn't need to say sorry, zip your lips.** As you read the following questions, remind children how to indicate their answers.

● **Would you say sorry if your mom bought you an ice-cream cone?**

● **Would you say sorry if you dropped your ice cream on your mom's lap?**

● **Would you say sorry if you and your friend were sharing a toy?**

● **Would you say sorry if you took a toy that wasn't yours?**

● **Would you say sorry if you went to the park with your family?**

● **Would you say sorry if you called your brother a mean name?**

Gather children in a circle and ask:

● **When should we tell someone we're sorry?** (When we hurt someone; if we do something naughty; if we're mean.)

● **What does it mean when we say sorry?** (That we wish we hadn't done it; that we feel bad about it; that we want to be forgiven.)

Say: **When we hurt someone or do something wrong,** Jesus wants us to be sorry. Let's read our Bible story about how Zacchaeus showed that he was sorry.

Bible Song and Prayer Time (up to 5 minutes)

Say: **Now it's time to choose a Bible person to bring me the Bible marked with today's Bible story. As we sing our Bible song, we'll pass around our special Bible. The person who's holding the Bible when the music stops will be our Bible person today.**

Lead children in singing "We Are Glad to Read the Bible" with the *cassette*

Jesus wants us to be sorry when we do wrong.

tape, to the tune of "Did You Ever See a Lassie?" As you sing, pass around the special Bible.

Sing

We are glad to read the Bible,
The Bible, the Bible.
We are glad to read the Bible
For it is God's Book.

We'll hear Bible stories
And learn about God's love.
We are glad to read the Bible
For it is God's Book.

When the music stops, invite the child who's holding the Bible to bring it to you. Stamp the child's hand with the *tree stamp* and thank the child for bringing you the Bible. Then stamp the other children's hands. Return the *tree stamp and ink pad* to the Learning Lab.

Say: **I'm thankful for** (name of child who brought the Bible) **and I'm thankful for everyone in our class today. Let's thank God together for all our friends in this class.**

Lead children in singing "We Are Glad to Pray Together" with the *cassette tape,* to the tune of "Did You Ever See a Lassie?" If you want to include the names of all the children in your class, sing the song without the cassette and repeat the naming section. If you choose to use the cassette, vary the names you use each week.

Sing

We are glad to pray together,
Together, together.
We are glad to pray together
And give thanks to God.

Lead children in folding their
hands and bowing their heads as
you continue to sing.

Thank you for (name),
And (name), and (name).
Thank you, God, for every person
Who's here in our class.

(Repeat)

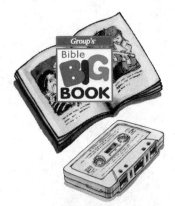

Hear the Bible Story (up to 8 minutes)

Form a circle and distribute the Zacchaeus finger puppets from Option 1.

Open the Bible to Luke 19 and show it to the children. Say: **Our Bible story comes from the book of Luke in the Bible.** Bring out the *Bible Big Book: Zacchaeus.* Say: **Our Bible Big Book shows us pictures of our Bible story. Let's listen to our story and hear what happened to Zacchaeus. Each time you hear the word "Jesus," run your Zacchaeus finger puppet up your arm to remember how Zacchaeus climbed up the tree to see Jesus.**

Hold the *Bible Big Book* so children can see it clearly. Play the "Zacchaeus" segment from the *cassette tape.* Follow along in the text printed on the back cover and turn the page when you hear the chime. When the story is over, turn off the cassette. Ask:

● **What bad things did Zacchaeus do?** (He took people's money; he took too much money.)

● **Why did Zacchaeus give the money back?** (He was sorry; he wanted to make Jesus happy; he felt bad about taking the money.)

● **How do you think people felt when they got their money back?**

Jesus wants us to be sorry when we do wrong.

(Surprised; happy; maybe they liked Zacchaeus; glad.)

Say:  **Jesus wants us to be sorry when we do wrong. Zacchaeus didn't just say he was sorry, he showed he was sorry by giving back the money he'd taken and by giving his things to poor people. When we do something wrong, it's important for us to show that we're sorry, not just say it. Now let's use our finger puppets as we sing a song about Zacchaeus and Jesus.**

The Point

Do the Bible Story (up to 5 minutes)

Form pairs and lead children in singing "Did You Ever See Zacchaeus?" to the tune of "Did You Ever See a Lassie?" with the *cassette tape*. Instruct one partner to hold his or her puppet up high, as if in a tree. The other partner can look at and point to the finger puppet during the song. Sing the song twice, allowing both partners to be the tree and Zacchaeus.

Sing

Did you ever see Zacchaeus (*hand over eyes across brow*),
Zacchaeus, Zacchaeus?
Did you ever see Zacchaeus
Way up in a tree? (*Point up high.*)

He looked 'round for Jesus (*turn around in a circle*),
Then climbed up to see him. (*Do climbing motions.*)
Did you ever see Zacchaeus (*hand over eyes across brow*)
Way up in a tree? (*Point up high.*)

Jesus saw Zacchaeus (*hand over eyes across brow*)
Zacchaeus, Zacchaeus.
Jesus saw Zacchaeus
Way up in that tree. (*Point up high.*)

"Zacchaeus, come down now." (*Wave towards self.*)
"I'm coming to your house." (*Point at another person.*)
Jesus saw Zacchaeus (*hand over eyes across brow*)
Way up in that tree. (*Point up high.*)

(Repeat)

Say: **Now use your Zacchaeus finger puppets to show your partner what Zacchaeus did when he came down from the tree.**

Allow a moment for children to show Zacchaeus giving his money away and showing that he loves Jesus. Then ask:

● **How can you show you're sorry when you've done something wrong?** (By giving a hug; by not doing it again; by helping clean up a mess I've made.)

● **How will people feel when you show you're sorry?** (Better; happy; glad.)

● **How will Jesus feel when you show you're sorry?** (Glad; happy.)

Say: **Zacchaeus showed that he was sorry by giving back the money he'd stolen.**  **Jesus wants us to be sorry, too. This week, when you do something wrong, remember to show that you're sorry. That makes everyone feel better! Let's see if Whiskers knows about saying, "I'm sorry."**

Collect the finger puppets and put them out of sight.

The Point

Practicing The Point

Sorry, Joey (up to 8 minutes)

Bring out Whiskers the Mouse holding a small toy truck between his paws and go through the following puppet script. When you finish the script, put Whiskers away and out of sight.

Sorry, Joey

PUPPET SCRIPT

Whiskers: Hi, everyone! I sure had fun sharing your snack last week. You were so kind to me. That's why I brought this toy truck to share with you!

Teacher: Wow! That's a nice truck, Whiskers. Where'd you get it?

Whiskers: It's my Cousin Joey's.

Teacher: Did Joey say that you could bring it here to share with us?

Whiskers: Well . . . no. He told me I couldn't play with it at all. But he's got so many great toys, I bet he doesn't even know I took it!

Teacher: Whiskers, it's wrong to take something that belongs to someone else. That's called stealing.

Whiskers: But I really, really like this truck! And . . . and I was going to let all my friends here use it, too!

Teacher: Children, I think Whiskers needs to hear about what Zacchaeus did.
   (*Allow children to tell how Zacchaeus took money from people and then returned all the money—plus four times more.*)

Whiskers: I guess I'm sorry that I took the truck. I just wanted to have something neat to share with everyone.

Teacher: Well, I'm glad you're sorry. But now you need to show Joey that you're sorry for taking his truck.

Whiskers: You mean by giving the truck back?

Teacher: I think that would be a good place to start!

Whiskers: OK, I'll take the truck back and tell Cousin Joey that I'm sorry for taking it. Maybe next week I can bring something of my own to share! 'Bye, everyone!

Jesus wants us to be sorry when we do wrong.

TODAY I LEARNED . . .

We believe Christian education extends beyond the classroom into the home. Photocopy the "Today I Learned..." handout (p. 180) for this week and send it home with your children. Encourage parents to use the handout to plan meaningful family activities to reinforce this week's topic. Follow up the "Today I Learned..." activities next week by asking children what their families did.

Closing

A Show of Hands (up to 5 minutes)

Say: **Whiskers did the right thing by returning the truck to his Cousin Joey. 🖊 Jesus wants us to be sorry when we do wrong, and it's important that we show we're sorry. Let's remember what Zacchaeus did to show that he was sorry for taking the people's money.**

Teach children the following finger play.

My name's Zacchaeus. I'm small as your thumb. *(Hold up your thumb.)*

I am a man Zacchaeus stole from. *(Hold up your pointer finger.)*

I'm the tall tree that Zacchaeus climbed. *(Hold up your middle finger.)*

My name is Jesus. I was loving and kind. *(Hold up your ring finger.)*

I'm the new Zacchaeus who learned right from wrong. *(Hold up your little finger.)*

Now everyone's glad to have me along! *(Wiggle all five fingers.)*

Repeat the rhyme a couple of times so children can learn the words. Then say: **🖊 Jesus wants us to be sorry when we do wrong. Let's pray and ask God to help us do that.** Pray: **Dear God, help us show we're sorry when we've done something wrong. Thank you for loving us and forgiving us. In Jesus' name, amen.**

🖊 **The Point**

🖊 **The Point**

For Extra Time

If you have a long class time or want to add additional elements to your lesson, try one of the following activities.

LIVELY LEARNING: Money Madness

Before class, hide 20 to 30 individually-wrapped candies around the room. Place a clean, empty jar in the middle of the room. On your signal, have children search for the candy and put it in the jar. As the jar fills up, explain that Zacchaeus showed he was sorry by giving back four times the amount of money he'd taken. Remind children that  Jesus wants us to be sorry when we do wrong.

MAKE TO TAKE: Coin Purses

Distribute paper plates and show children how to fold opposite edges in, as shown in the margin. Then have them fold the plates in half. Staple the sides, near the bottom, then punch two holes in the top edges and help children string a length of yarn through the holes. Be sure the yarn is long enough to allow children to pull the coin purses open. Allow children to decorate their coin purses with crayons, markers, and the *tree stamp*. As children work, review how Zacchaeus collected too much money from people, then gave back four times as much as he took. Remind them that 🖊 Jesus wants us to be sorry when we do wrong.

TREAT TO EAT: Money Bags

Set out spoons and bowls of ring-shaped cereal, such as Cheerios. Help each child pour four spoonfuls of cereal in a small bag. Tell children to pretend their bags of cereal are bags of coins. Encourage children to trade bags with someone else in the classroom. Remind them that Zacchaeus gave his money away.

STORY PICTURE: Zacchaeus Is Sorry

Give each child a photocopy of the "Today I Learned..." handout (p. 180). Set out glue sticks and small pieces of a brown grocery bag. Show children how to glue the brown paper on the money bags in the picture. As children work, ask them to tell you what Zacchaeus did with his money.

🖊 **The Point**

Jesus wants us to be sorry when we do wrong.

Zacchaeus Finger Puppet

Photocopy the handout and cut out the Zacchaeus puppets. Use a hole punch to make holes where children's fingers will go. Children will use a pencil or crayon to make the holes big enough for their fingers.

Permission to photocopy this handout from Group's Hands-On Bible Curriculum™ for Preschool granted for local church use.
Copyright © Group Publishing, Inc., Box 481, Loveland, CO 80539.

Jesus wants us to be sorry when we do wrong.

TODAY I LEARNED . . .

The Point ● Jesus wants us to be sorry when we do wrong.

Today your child learned that Jesus wants us to be sorry when we do wrong things. Children heard how Zacchaeus showed he was sorry for the wrong things he'd done. They talked about ways they can show they're sorry.

Verse to Learn

"Never become tired of doing good" (2 Thessalonians 3:13).

Ask Me . . .

● What had Zacchaeus done that was wrong?
● How did Zacchaeus show Jesus he was sorry?
● Tell about a time you showed that you were sorry.

Family Fun

● Make a family "Love Bank" by turning a plastic cup upside down and cutting a slit in the bottom. Cut out several small paper hearts and place them in a bowl next to the bank. When a family member apologizes or shows kindness, have him or her place a heart in the bank. When all the paper hearts have been deposited, celebrate with a visit to a frozen yogurt shop.

Zacchaeus Is Sorry (Luke 19:8)

Permission to photocopy this handout from Group's Hands-On Bible Curriculum™ for Preschool granted for local church use. Copyright © Group Publishing, Inc., Box 481, Loveland, CO 80539.

LESSON 12

Doin' It Right

The Point

✎ Jesus wants us to do what's right.

The Bible Basis

Luke 19:9-10. Zacchaeus learned right from wrong.

Zacchaeus' encounter with Jesus was life changing. Jesus' lovingkindness turned a selfish thief into a generous man who promised to give half his wealth to the poor and return four times more than what he'd taken. Jesus proclaimed that salvation had come to Zacchaeus' house because Zacchaeus chose to turn from sin and do what was right. Zacchaeus was lost in sin and greed, but Jesus found Zacchaeus and offered him forgiveness and a fresh start.

Jesus can change your preschoolers' lives, too! Children need Jesus' love and kindness, his gentle hand, and his comforting presence to guide them as they grow. Knowing and following Jesus will help children make wise decisions and choose to do what's right. Use this lesson to help children understand that Jesus wants all his followers, young and old, to do what's right.

Getting The Point

✎ **Jesus wants us to do what's right.**

It's important to say The Point just as it's written in each activity. Repeating The Point over and over will help the children remember it and apply it to their lives.

Children will
- hear how Zacchaeus did what was right,
- play a game to learn the difference between right and wrong,
- review the story of Zacchaeus, and
- understand that Jesus' love will help them do what's right.

⬤ **The Point**

This Lesson at a Glance

Before the lesson, collect the necessary items for the activities you plan to use. Refer to the Classroom Supplies and Learning Lab Supplies columns to determine what you'll need. Remember to make photocopies of the "Today I Learned . . ." handout (p. 192) to send home with your children.

Section	Minutes	What Children Will Do	Classroom Supplies	Learning Lab Supplies
Welcome Time	up to 5	**Welcome!**—Receive name tags and be greeted by the teacher.	"Angel Name Tags" hand-outs (p. 30)	
Let's Get Started Direct children to one or more of the Let's Get Started activities until everyone arrives.	up to 12	**Option 1: Puzzle Pieces**—Review the story of Zacchaeus by putting puzzles together.	Story Pictures from Lessons 10-13, poster board, glue, scissors, sack	
	up to 12	**Option 2: Four Times More**—Measure rice, then pour out four times more.	Uncooked rice, scoops, spoons, measuring cups, bowls	
	up to 12	**Option 3: Carrot Coin Counters**—Count carrot coins into bags.	Carrots, plastic bags, bowls, tray	
Pick-Up Song	up to 5	**Now It's Time**—Sing a song as they pick up toys and gather for Bible-Story Time.	Cassette player	Cassette: "Now It's Time"
Bible-Story Time	up to 5	**Setting the Stage**—Contribute their puzzle pieces to a group effort.	Story-Picture puzzles from Option 1, sack of puzzle pieces	
	up to 5	**Bible Song and Prayer Time**—Sing a song, bring out the Bible, and pray together.	Bible, cassette player	Tree stamp and ink pad, cassette: "We Are Glad . . ."
	up to 10	**Hear the Bible Story**—Listen carefully to the story of Zacchaeus from Luke 19:1-10 and correct the teacher's "mistakes."	Bible	Bible Big Book: Zacchaeus
	up to 5	**Do the Bible Story**—Decide which statements are right and wrong.		
Practicing The Point	up to 8	**Give It Away**—Help Whiskers learn ways to share God's love and do what's right.	Whiskers the Mouse, marshmallows, toys	
Closing	up to 5	**Handy Review**—Practice a finger play and pray.		
For Extra Time	For extra-time ideas and supplies, see page 191.			

Jesus wants us to do what's right.

Welcome Time

Welcome! (up to 5 minutes)

- Bend down and make eye contact with children as they arrive.
- Greet each child individually with an enthusiastic smile.
- Thank each child for coming to class today.
- As children arrive, ask them about last week's "Today I Learned..." discussion. Use questions such as "Did you tell anyone you were sorry this week? Tell me about it" and "How did you show that you were sorry?"
- Say: **Today we're going to learn that** 🖊 **Jesus wants us to do what's right.**
- Hand out the angel name tags children made during Lesson 1 and help them attach the name tags to their clothing. If some of the name tags were damaged or if children weren't in class that week, have them make new name tags using the photocopiable handout on page 30.
- Direct children to the Let's Get Started activities you've set up.

🖊 **The Point**

Let's Get Started

Set up one or more of the following activities for children to do as they arrive. After you greet each child, invite him or her to choose an activity.

Circulate among the children to offer help as needed and direct children's conversation toward the point of today's lesson. Ask questions such as "How do you feel when you do what's right?" and "How did Zacchaeus do what was right?"

OPTION 1: Puzzle Pieces (up to 12 minutes)

Before class, photocopy each of the Story Pictures from Lessons 10 through 13. Glue each picture to a different color of poster board, then cut the pictures into puzzles with about 10 pieces for each puzzle. When you cut the Story-Picture puzzle for Lesson 13, be sure to make enough puzzle pieces for each child in your class to have one piece.

Set out the Story-Picture puzzles for Lessons 10 through 12 and allow children to put them together. Place the Lesson 13 Story-Picture puzzle in a paper lunch sack and set it aside. As the children are putting the puzzles together, ask them to tell you what they remember about the story of Zacchaeus.

✔ If you have more than 10 children in your class, make two puzzles using the Story Picture from Lesson 13. Put each puzzle in a separate bag to use in Setting the Stage.

OPTION 2: Four Times More (up to 12 minutes)

Set out mixing bowls or shallow dishpans filled with several cups of uncooked rice. Provide scoops, spoons, ½-cup measuring cups, and empty bowls. Encourage children to measure and pour the rice. Measure out ½ cup of rice and then have children help you measure four more. Explain that Zacchaeus gave back four times the amount of the money that he'd stolen. Tell children that  Jesus wants us to do what's right.

 **The Point**

OPTION 3: Carrot Coin Counters (up to 12 minutes)

Before class, slice several small carrots into "coins." Set out plastic sandwich bags and bowls of carrot coins. Help children form an assembly line and make bags of carrot coins. Have each child add two coins to each bag. The last child in line may place the bags on a tray. As children work, explain that Zacchaeus did what was right when he gave his money to the poor and paid back the money he'd stolen. When children finish assembling their bags, they can eat the carrots or take them home. To prevent choking, encourage children to take several small bites from each coin.

When everyone has arrived and you're ready to move on to Bible-Story Time, encourage the children to finish what they're doing and get ready to clean up.

Pick-Up Song

Now It's Time (up to 5 minutes)

Lead children in singing "Now It's Time" with the *cassette tape,* to the tune of "The Mulberry Bush." Encourage children to sing along as they help clean up the room.

Sing

Now it's time to clean up our room,
Clean up our room,
Clean up our room.
Now it's time to clean up our room
And put our things away.

Will you help me? Yes, I will.
Yes, I will.
Yes, I will!
Will you help me? Yes, I will.
I'll help you right away.

(Repeat)

Jesus wants us to do what's right.

Bible-Story Time

Setting the Stage (up to 5 minutes)

Tell children that you'll clap three times to get their attention. Explain that when you clap three times, the children are to stop what they're doing and repeat the clap. Practice this signal a few times. Encourage children to respond quickly so you'll have time for all the fun activities you've planned.

Form a circle and ask:

● **What did you make or do when you came to class today?** (Put puzzles together; measured rice; made bags of carrot coins.)

Say: **If you put a puzzle together, hop to me and take a puzzle piece from this bag.** Pause while children follow your instructions. **If you measured rice, walk like a duck and take a puzzle piece.** Allow children to follow your instructions. **If you made bags of carrot coins, skip to me and take a puzzle piece.** When everyone has a puzzle piece, say: **Some of you put puzzles together, some of you measured things, and some of you made a snack we'll enjoy later. You were all learning important things about our Bible story. Let's see what we can remember about Zacchaeus.**

Hold up the first three Story Pictures and ask children to tell you what they remember about each one. Say: **We've learned a lot about Zacchaeus. I'd like to see what our last Story Picture looks like, wouldn't you? If each of you puts your puzzle piece in the middle of our circle, we can put this puzzle together and find out!**

Collect the pieces and have children work cooperatively to put the puzzle together. When the puzzle is complete, ask:

● **What's this a picture of?** (Zacchaeus giving back money; Zacchaeus being nice.)

● **How did we put this puzzle together?** (With everyone's pieces; by working together; by sharing our pieces.)

● **What if one person didn't give up his or her piece?** (The puzzle wouldn't be done; it would look funny; it wouldn't be right.)

Say: **You all did the right thing by sharing your puzzle pieces! Now we have a picture of Zacchaeus! In this picture, Zacchaeus is doing the right thing and giving back the money he took.** ◉ **Jesus wants us to do what's right. I'm proud that you all did what was right so we could put our puzzle together. Before we open our Bible and pray, let's clap because we all did the right thing!**

Bible Song and Prayer Time (up to 5 minutes)

Say: **Now it's time to choose a Bible person to bring me the Bible marked with today's Bible story. As we sing our Bible song, we'll pass around our special Bible. The person who's holding the Bible when the music stops will be our Bible person today.**

Lead children in singing "We Are Glad to Read the Bible" with the *cassette tape,* to the tune of "Did You Ever See a Lassie?" As you sing, pass around the special Bible.

◉ **The Point**

Jesus wants us to do what's right.

Sing

We are glad to read the Bible,
The Bible, the Bible.
We are glad to read the Bible
For it is God's Book.

We'll hear Bible stories
And learn about God's love.
We are glad to read the Bible
For it is God's Book.

When the music stops, invite the child who's holding the Bible to bring it to you. Stamp the child's hand with the *tree stamp* and thank the child for bringing you the Bible. Then stamp the other children's hands. Return the *tree stamp and ink pad* to the Learning Lab.

Say: **I'm thankful for** (name of child who brought the Bible) **and I'm thankful for everyone in our class today. Let's thank God together for all our friends in this class.**

Lead children in singing "We Are Glad to Pray Together" with the *cassette tape*, to the tune of "Did You Ever See a Lassie?" If you want to include the names of all the children in your class, sing the song without the cassette and repeat the naming section. If you choose to use the cassette, vary the names you use each week.

Sing

We are glad to pray together,
Together, together.
We are glad to pray together
And give thanks to God.

Lead children in folding their
hands and bowing their heads as
you continue to sing.

Thank you for (name),
And (name), and (name).
Thank you, God, for every person
Who's here in our class.

(Repeat)

Hear the Bible Story (up to 10 minutes)

Bring out the *Bible Big Book: Zacchaeus.* Have children gather around you. Say: **Our Bible story comes from the book of Luke in the Bible. Our *Bible Big Book* shows us pictures of our Bible story. We've read this story for three weeks. Let's see if you can catch any mistakes in the story I'm reading and then tell me what the story should say. Clap your hands every time you hear a mistake.** Show the children the pictures in the *Bible Big Book*, but use the text printed below.

✔ All of the "wrong words" are capitalized within the story text as it's written for you here. Tell the story slowly and distinctly, allowing time for the children to catch your "mistakes."

Page 1

Hi! My name is Zacchaeus. Even though I'm a grown-up, I'm very TALL. I have to climb up on a HORSE to reach things in my house. And when I'm in a crowd of people, I can't see anything at all! But I don't mind my size so much because I have a very important job. I get to go to people's

houses and collect FOOD for taxes. I'm supposed to give all the FOOD to the government, but I usually take extra money and keep it for myself. I may be TALL, but I sure am rich! Can you help me count my money?

Pages 2-3

When I was sitting at my booth collecting taxes this morning, I heard lots of DINOSAURS saying that Jesus is planning to visit our town today! I've heard that Jesus can do great miracles. I sure would like to see him. Look! Here he comes down the road!

Wow! Look at all the people! Everyone in town must have come to see Jesus. I wish I weren't so BIG and TALL—I'll never be able to see Jesus over all these people. Everybody is standing BEHIND me, and they won't let me through. What can I do?

Pages 4-5

Hmm. There's a sycamore tree up ahead. If I climb that tree, I'll be able to see Jesus. Oh yes! I can see everything from DOWN here. There's Jesus, and he's coming this way!

Oh my! Jesus is looking up at me! I don't know how he knew I was up here, but I'm SAD he found me. He's smiling at me. What? Jesus wants to come to my SCHOOL BUS! Wow, no one has ever wanted to come to my house before. I'd better hurry home to get ready for Jesus.

Pages 6-7

Listen to all the people complaining about me. All the way home I heard people complaining about me. "Doesn't Jesus know Zacchaeus steals our FOOD?" "Why does Jesus want to visit him?" I wonder if Jesus will change his mind about coming to my house. No, he's still following me. Oh, I'm so glad. I'll fix Jesus a nice BATH.

I can tell that Jesus loves me very much. I'm so sorry for taking other people's SHOES. I know what I'll do! I'll give back even more money than I stole in the first place. Now that I have Jesus' love in my heart, I want to do what's right. Jesus wants you to do what's right, too. Can you do that?

Page 8

Tomorrow I'll start visiting all the people I've stolen CANDY BARS from. They may not want to talk to me. But I'll tell them I'm sorry, and that from now on I'll do what's right. I'll give back all the money I took, and even more. Then they'll see that from now on I'm going to be loving and kind, just like Jesus.

Close the book and say: **Thank you for helping me tell the Bible story the right way!** Ask:
● **What bad things did Zacchaeus do?** (He took money; he stole; he was mean.)
● **What good things did Zacchaeus do?** (He was friends with Jesus; he gave the money back; he gave to poor people.)
Say: ✏ **Jesus wants us to do what's right, just like Zacchaeus did. Now let's all practice doing what's right!**

⬤ The Point

Jesus wants us to do what's right.

Do the Bible Story (up to 5 minutes)

Say: **We're going to play a game to help remember what's right and what's wrong. I'll say some good things to do and some bad things. When I say a good thing, jump up and say "right." Let's try that right now. Right!** (Pause.) **When I say a bad thing, shake your head and say "wrong." Let's try that, too. Wrong!** (Pause.)

Read the following list, allowing time for children to respond.

- **I'll sing a song to show Jesus I love him.**
- **I'm going to hit my friend because he was mean to me.**
- **My friend looks sad, so I'm going to cheer her up.**
- **I wish I had a truck like Tommy's, so I'm going to take his truck away.**
- **I'm going to help my sister pick up her toys.**
- **I'm going to yell at everyone because I'm so tired.**
- **My mom looks tired, so I'm going to give her a hug.**

 **The Point**

Say:  **Jesus wants us to do what's right. You did a great job of telling what was right and what was wrong. Now you can do what's right and hide your eyes, and I'll bring out a special friend to visit you.**

Practicing The Point

Give It Away (up to 8 minutes)

Place a bag of marshmallows and several toys and stuffed animals in a paper grocery sack. Set the sack near your story area.

Bring out Whiskers the Mouse and go through the following puppet script. When you finish the script, put Whiskers away and out of sight.

Give It Away
PUPPET SCRIPT

Teacher: Open your eyes and see who's here. Hi, Whiskers. How are you?

Whiskers: I'm super stupendous! And I even brought a surprise for everyone!

Teacher: A surprise? What is it?

Whiskers: It's in that bag over there. Open it up and look inside!

Teacher: (Opens bag and looks inside.) Wow! Whiskers, what is all this stuff? Did you take toys from someone else again?

Whiskers: Nope! These are all my toys! Everything I have! I want to give them all away to my friends.

Teacher: Why do you want to give all of your things away?

Whiskers: Well, because that's the right thing to do! Didn't Zacchaeus give all his stuff away?

(Continued)

Jesus wants us to do what's right.

Teacher: Children, who can tell Whiskers what Zacchaeus gave away?

(Allow children to tell about how Zacchaeus gave half of his money to the poor people. They can also tell Whiskers that Zacchaeus gave back four times the amount of money that he stole.)

Whiskers: Oh, I get it. Zacchaeus gave back what he took. That was the right thing to do. Hmm, maybe I could share some of my things, just like Zacchaeus did. *(Pulls out a bag of marshmallows.)* I could share these!

Teacher: Good idea, Whiskers. Jesus is happy when we share. Zacchaeus showed Jesus' love by giving away the things that had kept him from loving others. *(Distribute marshmallows.)* Children, who can tell other things we can do to show Jesus' love? *(Children may say things such as praying, going to church, or being kind to others.)*

Whiskers: Those are great ideas! I'm gonna go tell Cousin Joey that ✏ Jesus wants us to do what's right. And I'll share my marshmallows with him, too.

Teacher: That sounds good to me, Whiskers. Don't forget to take your toys!

Whiskers: I won't! 'Bye, everyone! Thanks for helping me learn how to do what's right!

✏ **The Point**

TODAY I LEARNED . . .

We believe Christian education extends beyond the classroom into the home. Photocopy the "Today I Learned..." handout (p. 192) for this week and send it home with your children. Encourage parents to use the handout to plan meaningful family activities to reinforce this week's topic. Follow up the "Today I Learned..." activities next week by asking children what their families did.

Closing

Handy Review (up to 5 minutes)

Say: **Remember the finger play we learned last week? Let's say that again so you can tell the story of Zacchaeus to your family and friends.**
Lead children in the following finger play:
My name's Zacchaeus. I'm small as your thumb. *(Hold up your thumb.)*
I am a man Zacchaeus stole from. *(Hold up your pointer finger.)*
I'm the tall tree that Zacchaeus climbed. *(Hold up your middle finger.)*

Jesus wants us to do what's right.

My name is Jesus. I was loving and kind. *(Hold up your ring finger.)*

I'm the new Zacchaeus who learned right from wrong. *(Hold up your little finger.)*

Now everyone's glad to have me along! *(Wiggle all five fingers.)*

Ask:

● **Why didn't people like Zacchaeus?** (He took their money; he didn't love Jesus; he wasn't kind.)

● **Why do you think they like Zacchaeus now?** (He learned to love Jesus; he gave their money back; he was kind to the poor.)

🖊 The Point

Say: 🖊 **Jesus wants us to do what's right. Zacchaeus used to do wrong things. But when he found Jesus' love, Zacchaeus learned to do what was right. Let's pray and ask Jesus to help us do what's right, too.**

Pray: **Dear God, thank you for your kindness and for teaching us to be sorry when we do wrong things. Help us learn to do what's right, just like Zacchaeus did. Amen.**

For Extra Time

If you have a long class time or want to add additional elements to your lesson, try one of the following activities.

LIVELY LEARNING: Review With Whiskers

Bring out Whiskers and the *Bible Big Book: Zacchaeus*. As you read the story to children, have Whiskers ask questions such as "Was Zacchaeus as small as I am?" "Why did Zacchaeus do bad things?" or "Does Jesus love me as much as he loved Zacchaeus?" Invite children to respond to Whiskers' questions.

MAKE TO TAKE: Hidden Pictures

Have children draw a picture of Zacchaeus on white paper, using a white crayon. Point out how hard it is to see the drawing. Then allow children to paint over their pictures with watercolor paints. The white crayon will resist the paint and cause the drawing of Zacchaeus to appear. Remind children that Jesus found Zacchaeus and taught him to do what's right.

TREAT TO EAT: Lost and Found

Set out your choice of snack foods such as peanuts, raisins, oat-ring cereal, pumpkin seeds, or dried fruit. Have children measure four spoonfuls of each item into plastic bags. Then have children close their eyes while you push a Hershey's Kiss into the middle of each bag. Ask children if they can dig through the bag to find the special surprise hidden in their snack. Remind children that Zacchaeus found Jesus' love and it helped him to do what's right.

STORY PICTURE: Zacchaeus Does What's Right

Give each child a copy of the "Today I Learned..." handout (p. 192). Set out crayons and glitter glue. After children have colored their pictures, help them place a drop of glitter glue on each coin. As children work, review the story of Zacchaeus and remind them that ◓ Jesus wants us to do what's right.

◓ **The Point**

Jesus wants us to do what's right.

TODAY I LEARNED . . .

The Point 🔖 Jesus wants us to do what's right.

Today your child learned that Jesus wants us to do what's right. Children heard how Jesus forgave Zacchaeus for the wrong things he'd done and that Zacchaeus gave half his money to the poor and paid back four times what he'd stolen. They asked God to help them do what's right, too.

Verse to Learn

"Never become tired of doing good" (2 Thessalonians 3:13).

Ask Me . . .

● How did Zacchaeus learn to do what's right?
● What things can I do that would make Jesus happy?
● Who helps us do what's right?

Family Fun

● Take a "Right-Way Walk" around your neighborhood. Each time you come to a corner or intersection, describe a situation in which a family member must choose to do right or wrong. If that member chooses to do what's right, continue your walk to the right. If he or she chooses to do what's wrong, turn to the left. As you walk, think of ways to help each other do what's right.

Zacchaeus Does What's Right (Luke 19:9-10)

Permission to photocopy this handout from Group's Hands-On Bible Curriculum™ for Preschool granted for local church use. Copyright © Group Publishing, Inc., Box 481, Loveland, CO 80539.